Campus Women Face Sexual Violence

Brent H. Dashiell
All Rights Reserved

Abstract

Sexual violence (SV) is a profound and widespread public health problem and is the most common type of violence experienced by students in higher education. Approximately one in five college women experience sexual violence, despite decades of prevention efforts. College sexual violence results in many physical and psychological consequences, often leading to academic failure and altering survivors' entire life trajectories

This qualitative, descriptive study, guided by the socioecological model, aimed to provide an in-depth understanding of college sexual violence as described by female survivors. The research questions that guided the study were: How do college women describe college SV experiences within a socioecological framework of intrapersonal, interpersonal, institutional, community, and societal factors; and how may women's college SV experiences inform college sexual violence prevention and intervention? The data for this study were extracted from a single account on a social media site, Instagram, created by one or more sexual violence activist(s). Eight hundred and ninety one (N = 891) posts were analyzed in an iterative five-cycle inductive and deductive process. Analysis of the final study sample, three hundred eighty-four (N =384) college women's experiences of sexual violence, revealed seven themes, including subthemes, that represent the experiences of the survivors.

This study's findings open several potential pathways to strengthen primary prevention programs and post-assault support and intervention at each level of the socioecological model. Findings support existing literature on college sexual violence and offer new information that requires further research and attention from institutions, communities, and policymakers. In addition, the study's findings underscore the need for programs that educate and improve societal attitudes toward sexual violence. Practice implications and future directions for research and policy are presented.

Acknowledgements

I would like to extend my deepest appreciation and gratitude to my dissertation committee for their support and guidance throughout this process. To Dr. Melissa Sutherland, my success would not have been possible without your invaluable suggestions and insight. Your encouragement and patience helped me land the plane; I would have been on a never-ending flight without you. To Dr. Pamela Stewart Fahs, I am incredibly grateful for your kindness and patience. To Dr. Nicole Rouhana, thank you for always making me feel supported and valued. Also, I would like to thank Dr. Rodney Gabel for enthusiastically agreeing to be my outside reader. Many faculty and staff have contributed to my professional growth during my graduate studies and offered support and encouragement through this journey. A special thank you to Dr. Serdar Atav, Dr. Rosemary Collier, Dr. Rosa Darling, and Dr. Jodi Sutherland for your mentorship and friendship. You have each contributed to my professional growth and provided invaluable support and encouragement throughout this journey. My research was made possible through grants from Sigma Theta Tau, Zeta Iota Chapter, and Binghamton University Women, Gender, and Sexuality Studies.

My biggest thank you goes to my family. Daniel and Morgan, thank you for your support and understanding while I completed this academic journey that has lasted most of your life. I promise not to say "I am busy" next time you call. Paul, my biggest supporter and fan, I could never have accomplished this goal without your endless love, encouragement, and support. I will be forever grateful for the day our paths crossed.

Table of Contents

List of Figures x

List of Abbreviations xi

Chapter 1: Introduction 1

    Overview of the Study 1

    Conceptual Framework 8

Chapter 2: Literature Review 12

    Background and Significance 12

    Definitions 14

    Prevalence 15

    Risk Factors 18

    Activism 48

    Summary 50

Chapter 3: Methodology 52

    Setting 53

    Human Subjects Protection 54

    Data Collection 54

    Data Sample 55

    Data Analysis 56

    Rigor and Trustworthiness 59

    Summary 61

Chapter 4: Findings 62

    Data Findings and Analysis 62

    Thematic Findings 63

Chapter 5: Discussion 83

    Problem Statement 84

    Summary of Thematic Findings and the Literature 85

    Implications of this Study 96

    Application of the Socioecological Model 103

    Strengths and Limitations 105

    Conclusion 106

List of Figures

Figure 1. Ecological Model..11

Figure 2. Five-cycle Data Analysis..58

Figure 3. Approach to Prevention and Intervention..104

List of Abbreviations

SV   Sexual violence

SEM   Socioecological Model

RA   Resident Assistant

Chapter 1: Introduction

Overview of the Study

Approximately one in five college women experience college sexual violence (SV) despite decades of prevention efforts (Koss et al., 2014; Muehlenhard et al., 2017; White House Task Force to Protect Students from Sexual Assault, 2017). The Centers for Disease Control and Prevention (Basile et al., 2014) defined SV as a sexual act committed or attempted without the freely given consent of the victim or against someone who refuses or is unable to consent. Sexual violence includes both penetrative and nonpenetrative acts as well as noncontact acts. Sexual violence has been the most common type of violence experienced by students in higher education (Bhochhibhoya et al., 2021; Scribner et al., 2010). College women experience SV significantly more than college men and therefore were the focus of the study (Bhochhibhoya et al., 2021; J. C. Campbell et al., 2021; Herres et al., 2018).

Koss et al. (1987) were the first to estimate the national scope of SV prevalence on college campuses. Since then, the estimated prevalence of SV on college campuses has increased (Cantor et al., 2020; Koss et al., 2022). Researchers have estimated the economic burden of this preventable public health problem to be over three trillion dollars (Peterson et al., 2017; Potter et al., 2018), and the effects of college SV on survivors may last for years, altering their entire life trajectories (Potter et al., 2018). Capturing the true scope of the problem has been challenging because of variations in terminology, methodology, campus reporting, and disclosure (Fedina et al., 2018; Halstead et al., 2017; Weiss & Lasky, 2017).

No consensus has emerged regarding the definition of SV and its components (Basile & Smith, 2011), which has contributed to inconsistencies in SV research methods (Rueff & Gross, 2017) and outcomes (Fedina et al., 2018; Koss, 1993; Krause et al., 2018; Krebs, 2014). The Sexual Experiences Survey, developed by Koss and Oros (1982), is a self-report survey instrument frequently used to estimate the prevalence of college SV. The Sexual Experiences Survey has undergone modification since its initial development to reflect changes in legal definitions of attempted rape and rape; however, the instrument does not use the term *rape* or *attempted rape* (Koss et al., 2007). Researchers using the Sexual Experiences Survey in prevalence studies have modified the instrument, resulting in variability in labeling SV occurrences (Halstead et al., 2017; Koss et al., 2007). Definitions used by colleges to guide SV policies, campus climate surveys, and reporting procedures also vary significantly from institution to institution (Moylan et al., 2019; Sabina & Ho, 2014; Weiss & Lasky, 2017). Researchers have suggested that standardizing definitions would improve prevalence estimates and increase rates of institutional reporting and disclosure by survivors (Gronert, 2019; Koss et al., 2022; Rueff & Gross, 2017).

Multiple factors, some of which intersect and cannot be changed, place women at elevated risk of college SV. Factors contributing to SV on college campuses include gender (Bhochhibhoya et al., 2021; J. C. Campbell et al., 2021; Cantor et al., 2020; Mellins et al., 2017; Wood et al., 2018), year of enrollment (Cantor et al., 2020; Cranney, 2015; Flack et al., 2008; Krebs et al., 2016), alcohol use (Caamano-Isorna et al., 2018;

Ford et al., 2021), campus demographics (Wiersma-Mosley et al., 2017), prior victimization (Caamano-Isorna et al., 2018), and involvement in campus organizations and groups (Wiersma-Mosley et al., 2017).

In response to college SV, the Sexual Assault Violence Elimination Act, signed by President Obama in 2013, mandated that universities participating in Title IX federal financial programs provide students, faculty, and staff members with SV primary prevention and awareness programs (DeMaria et al., 2015; Orchowski et al., 2018). Prevention education programs aimed at decreasing the prevalence of college SV fall mainly into the categories of risk reduction and primary prevention (American College Health Association [ACHA], 2020; DeGue, Valle et al., 2014; Orchowski et al., 2018). Risk reduction programs provide information and strategies for threat deterrence, boundary setting, and self-defense; expand knowledge about sexual desires, relationship values, and negotiation skills; and identify barriers to the acknowledgment of risk (Orchowski et al., 2018). The elements of primary prevention programs focus on individual and campus community education to change rape culture, influence social norms, encourage healthy masculinity, and provide bystander education (ACHA, 2020). Prevention program development has received guidance from theory (e.g., socioecology, the theory of planned behavior, social change theory, and social norm theory; Banyard, 2014; Coker et al., 2017; DeGue, Valle et al., 2014), known risk factors, and known characteristics of perpetrators of violence (Coker et al., 2017). Researchers evaluating college SV prevention have overwhelmingly measured outcomes through self-reported changes in attitude (Banyard, 2014) and behavioral intent rather than actual behavior or behavioral change (Schulze & Budd, 2020). Furthermore, researchers have not adequately addressed the value of college SV survivors' experiences informing the development and evaluation of SV prevention programs.

Researchers examining college SV disclosure have shown survivors are more likely to disclose informally to friends and family than formally to campus authorities or police (Sabri et al., 2019). An estimated 25%–55% of survivors never disclose their experiences to anyone (Orchowski & Gidycz, 2012). Barriers to formal disclosure described by survivors include campus policy and reporting procedures (Bloom et al., 2022; Gronert, 2019), concerns around confidentiality and disciplinary action (Sabina & Ho, 2014; Sabri et al., 2019), cultural scripts and norms (Ahrens et al., 2010), prior victimization (Orchowski & Gidycz, 2012), involvement of alcohol or drugs (Kilpatrick et al., 2007; Sabri et al., 2019); and self-blame (Carey et al., 2018; Holland & Cortina, 2017; Zinzow & Thompson, 2011).

Although campus prevention efforts focus on stopping SV before it happens, campus intervention focuses on supporting survivors in the aftermath of SV. Formal support options for SV survivors can be institution-based (e.g., Title IX offices, sexual assault centers, counseling and health service centers, faculty, and housing staff) or community-based (e.g., police, community rape and crisis centers, sexual assault nurse examiners, and community hospitals). Despite the number of available formal support services, few college SV survivors seek assistance (R. Campbell et al., 2008; Sabina & Ho, 2014). Support provided by a survivor's friends, family members, or significant other is a form of informal support. More recent research has investigated the support provided online via social media (Facebook, Twitter, and Instagram) as compared with face-to-face/in-person support (Men, few college SV survivors seek assistance (R. Campbell et al., 2008; Sabina & Ho, 2014). Support provided by a survivor's friends, family members, or significant other is a form of informal support. More recent research has investigated the support provided online via social media (Facebook, Twitter, and Instagram) as compared with face-to-face/in-person support (Mendes et al., 2018).

Survivors of SV have reported a mixture of positive and negative reactions to a disclosure (Ahrens et al., 2010; R. Campbell et al., 2008). Survivors who receive positive support following disclosure, formally or informally, report enhanced self-worth (Littleton & Breitkopf, 2006) and improved mental health (Ahrens et al., 2010; S. E. Ullman, 1999). However, survivors who receive poor social support following SV may experience self-blame, use alcohol to cope (S. E. Ullman et al., 2008), and experience poor psychological outcomes (Edwards, Waterman et al., 2020; Hawn et al., 2018), which in turn increases the risk of revictimization (Hawn et al., 2018).

The immediate and long-term consequences of college SV can be mild or severe, physical and/or psychological, and often lead to academic failure (Banyard et al., 2017; Potter et al., 2018; Sutherland et al., 2021). Negative psychological consequences of college SV include posttraumatic stress disorder (PTSD; Eisenberg et al., 2016; Krebs et al., 2016), major depression (R. Campbell et al., 2008; Eisenberg et al., 2016), anxiety (Eisenberg et al., 2016), suicidal ideation (Chang et al., 2015), and alcohol and substance abuse (Rothman et al., 2021). College SV survivors have reported immediate physical problems (e.g., broken bones, bruises, and vaginal tears) and reproductive health conditions (e.g., sexually transmitted diseases and unwanted pregnancy; Basile et al., 2021; Cantor et al., 2020; Farahi & McEachern, 2021; Potter et al., 2018). The mental and physical stress on survivors affects academic performance, resulting in poor class attendance, difficulty concentrating (Cantor et al., 2020; Jordan et al., 2014), lowered grades (Brewer et al., 2018; Potter et al., 2018), and reduced likelihood of graduation (Banyard et al., 2017; Potter et al., 2018).

Changes in public and university policy responses to college SV have largely been prompted by student and SV survivor-led activism (Bovill et al., 2021; Eriksen et al., 2022). Student and SV survivor activists have organized on-campus events (e.g., Take Back the Night marches and Mattress Performance [Carry that Weight]) off-campus organizations (e.g., Know Your IX and SurvJustice), and online platforms (e.g., Project Unbreakable, Surviving in Numbers, It Happens Here) in response to college SV (Bovill et al., 2021; Driessen, 2020; Eriksen et al., 2022). Additionally, *The Hunting Ground* is a documentary describing the efforts of two survivor student activists who traveled nationally helping other survivors file complaints to the U.S. Department of Education's Office for Civil Rights against their institution's handling of SV (Bovill et al., 2021). As a result of their efforts, the office reviewed over 287 complaints filed by students between 2011 and 2016 Activism by college students and survivors has challenged rape culture, increased awareness of SV, supported survivors who disclose their experiences, and demanded action and policy change from institutions and governments (Bovill et al., 2021; Eriksen et al., 2022).

Despite decades of research, federal mandates, prevention efforts, and activism, college SV has remained a complex and persistent public health problem. Barriers to disclosure have persisted, and surveys do not allow survivors to tell their individual stories of SV. College SV prevention programs have proliferated, developed by researchers, colleges, and external organizations, although none have demonstrated a reduction in the prevalence of SV (Mujal et al., 2019; C. Ullman, 2020; Worthen & Wallace, 2018). The development and evaluation of college SV prevention programs must prioritize student and survivor voices (Bloom et al., 2022; Krause et al., 2018; McMahon et al., 2021; Sabri et al., 2019) and include a detailed understanding of individual campus demographics based on existing data or other innovative approaches (DeGue, Fowler & Randall, 2014; Dills et al., 2016; Fedina et al., 2018). Women who have experienced college SV have had little to no voice in the development or evaluation of college SV prevention programs, although SV survivors do want the opportunity to share their experiences and contribute to violence prevention (Bloom et al., 2022; R. Campbell & Adams, 2009; Jaffe et al., 2017).

Accordingly, the aims of this qualitative descriptive study were to (a) describe the stories of female survivors of SV at a public university and (b) examine the survivors' experiences of SV framed within the socioecological model (SEM). The following research questions guided the study:

1. How do college women describe college SV experiences within a socioecological framework of intrapersonal, interpersonal, institutional, community, and societal factors?
2. How may women's college SV experiences inform college SV prevention and intervention programs?

Examining survivor experiences provided insight into effective and ineffective methods of college SV prevention and intervention. The outcomes of this study contribute to the college SV literature by providing insight into, and relevant knowledge of, college SV prevention and intervention programs, disclosure, risk factors, and consequences of SV from female survivors' perspectives, confirming what is known and identifying areas for improvement and future research. Finally, this study gave a voice to female survivors who have chosen to disclose their experiences of college SV.

Conceptual Framework

The CDC, World Health Organization, ACHA, and key SV organizations (e.g., Washington Coalition of Sexual Assault Programs and National Sexual Violence Resource Center) have adopted and promoted the SEM to better understand violence (McMahon et al., 2021). The SEM is a health behavior model that accounts for multiple levels of influence. According to the model, an individual's well-being depends on complex relations of their immediate settings, formal and informal social structures, societal norms, and institutional patterns (Bronfenbrenner, 1977). Bronfenbrenner (1977) postulated that in the ecological model, human development is shaped in the environments that humans create. The socio-cultural environment and physical environment are factors that cross each level (Sallis et al., 2015).

An ecological approach focuses on both population- and individual-level influences on behavior and health and guides multilevel prevention and intervention. Underlying the ecological perspective is the basic assumption that health encompasses physical health, emotional well-being, and social cohesion (Stokols, 1992). A fundamental strength of the SEM is the ability it provides to focus on multiple levels of influence, thus creating more opportunities for intervention development. The five core principles of the model are as follows (Sallis et al., 2015):

- Multiple levels of influence exist, including factors at the intrapersonal, interpersonal, organizational, community, and public policy levels.

- Environmental contexts are significant determinants of health behavior.
- Influences on behaviors interact across these different levels.
- Ecological models should be behavior specific, identifying the most relevant potential influences at each level.
- Multilevel interventions should be the most effective for changing behavior.

The ACHA (2020) adapted the five-leveled SEM to improve student, faculty, and staff health (Figure 1). The ecological approach is useful to identify environmental factors and influences, which interact with and affect individual behavior. McLeroy et al., (1988) posited patterned behavior is the outcome of interest and is determined by the following:

- Intrapersonal: individual characteristics that contribute to an individual's knowledge, self-concept, skills, and developmental history. This includes biologic sex, sexual orientation, access to services, perceptions of social norms, rape myth attitudes, and trauma history.
- Interpersonal: processes and primary groups, formal and informal networks, and social support systems such as relationships with family, peers, or friends. This level includes roommates, resident assistants, athletics, Greek life, active bystander behavior, and peer norms related to sexual respect.
- Institutional: factors and influences, formal and informal rules, and regulations for operation. This includes campus climate, design and staffing of social spaces on campus, policies, and communication of those policies, such as amnesty related to alcohol use, definition of consent, confidential and culturally sensitive recourses, and collaboration among prevention educators,

advocates, law enforcement, Title IX, and conduct and student support services.

- Community: relationships among organizations, institutions, and informal networks within defined boundaries. Include at this level are location in the community, built environment, neighborhood associations, housing, community businesses such as bars, transportation, design and staffing of social spaces off campus, law enforcement, campus community relationships, and medical and mental health services.

- Public policy: state, local, and national laws, and policies. This includes policies that provide resources connecting individuals to the larger social community to create a healthy campus. For example, laws regarding alcohol sales, violence, and social justice, Title IX, the Clery Act, Violence Against Women, Campus SaVE Act.

The ecological approach for prevention of college SV structures risk and protective factors within the context of intrapersonal factors, interpersonal processes and primary groups, institutional factors, community factors, and public policy. This approach allows for systematic assessment of the interaction between individual levels and community levels of influence on all factors (e.g., risk, prevention, disclosure, and intervention) related to college SV.

Figure 1

Ecological Approach

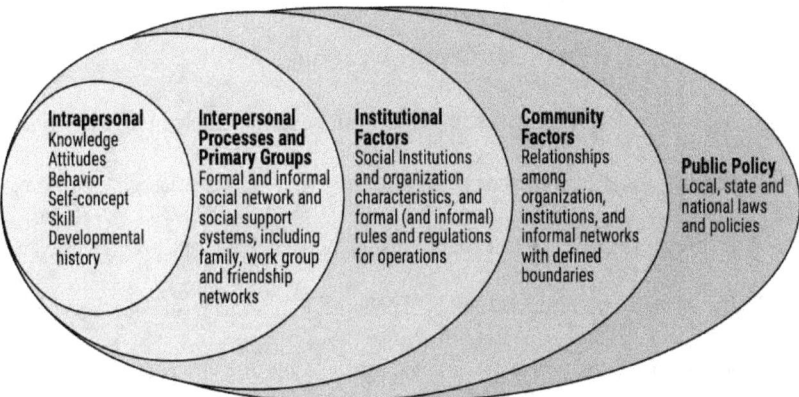

Note. See ACHA (2020)

In this study, utilization of the SEM supports maintaining a substantial positive understanding of college SV through the lens of individual, environmental/societal, and policy level factors. Influencing large populations requires interventions implemented through policy at the environmental and societal levels rather than at the individual level (Sallis et al., 2015). The SEM guided this study and informed the primary investigators (PI) understanding of survivors' experiences of college SV through multiple levels of the social ecology.

Chapter 2: Literature Review

This chapter provides an overview of the state of science regarding SV on college campuses, starting with a comprehensive review of factors influencing the development of college SV prevention and intervention programs. The chapter continues with discussion of the historical context of college SV, risk factors of college SV, college SV prevention programs, factors surrounding disclosure of SV, support for survivors, and consequences of college SV.

Background and Significance

Sexual violence (SV) is a profound and widespread public health issue and has been the most common type of violence experienced by students in higher education (Scribner et al., 2010; Sinozich & Langton, 2014). Although campus SV has been vastly underreported, researchers studying its prevalence have found that approximately 20%–25% of women experience SV while in college (Fedina et al., 2018; Fisher et al., 2000). The limited disclosure of college SV has implications not only for prevalence but also for prevention, institutional support, and the ability to fully comprehend the complexities of college SV and its negative influence on survivors' health and well-being. Over the last 10 years, grassroots activism by students and survivors has brought significant attention to college SV. Obama administration mandates—such as the Dear Colleague Letter, the Clery Act, and Campus SaVE projects—amplified this attention (Eriksen et al., 2022). Despite activism by college students and SV survivors, risk reduction education, and primary prevention programs, the prevalence of college SV has increased since Koss et al. (1987) conducted the first study to capture the national scope of the problem (Cantor et al., 2020; Koss et al., 2022).

Researchers investigating college SV have primarily focused on understanding the help-seeking behaviors of victims, identifying SV outcomes, analyzing risk and protective factors, and examining prevalence rates (Moylan & Javorka, 2020). Few researchers have attempted to capture survivors' experiences of college SV qualitatively. In 2020, C. Ullman interviewed SV survivors ($N = 19$) to understand what justice meant to them; they overwhelmingly described justice as prevention of sexual assault from happening to someone else. Karunaratne and Harris (2022) conducted a qualitative study of the perceptions of female student survivors of color ($N = 44$) regarding institutional campus sexual assault prevention programming. The participants' perceptions of online training, presentations during new student orientation, and who perpetrates sexual assault suggested that college SV prevention programs were not engaging or effective, fell short of program aims, and did not reflect the context of the institution.

As part of a larger study on college SV, Sabri et al. (2019) applied the SEM to a qualitative investigation of survivors' perspectives on primary and secondary prevention. Participants ($N = 21$) described barriers to reporting SV and seeking services following assault: concern about their stories not being believed, personal minimization of incidents, belief that no action would result from reporting, confidentiality, and perceived costs of reporting (e.g., social and personal). Participants' recommendations for primary prevention included social media programming, increased access to confidential services through different formats (e.g., phone, office, and online) and longer hours, multiple programs over time, bystander training encompassing how to respond, peer disclosure models, and self-help kits for preservation of evidence. As these findings illustrate, survivors of college SV can provide valuable insight into prevention and intervention programs offered at their institution and contribute to the primary goal of preventing college SV.

Definitions

Authors often use the terms *sexual assault, rape,* and *interpersonal violence* interchangeably, and definitions have varied among studies of college SV (Fedina et al., 2018; Krause et al., 2018). Krause et al. (2018) conducted a systematic review of 107 campus climate survey reports and found a wide variation in how colleges and universities defined sexual assault. Fedina et al. (2018) reviewed 35 independent studies of college SV and reported considerable variation in sexual assault definitions and measurement tools.

According to the Office for Civil Rights (2011), SV consists of physical and sexual acts perpetrated against a person's will or when a person is incapable of giving consent due to the use of drugs or alcohol or due to an intellectual or other disability. Sexual acts include rape, sexual assault, sexual battery, sexual abuse, and sexual coercion. According to the World Health Organization (2012), acts that range from verbal harassment to forced penetration, various types of coercive acts such as intimidation to social pressure fall under the umbrella term SV. The CDC defines SV as a sexual act committed or attempted without the freely given consent of the victim or against someone who refuses or is unable to consent; SV includes both penetrative and nonpenetrative acts and noncontact acts (Basile et al., 2014). This study adopted the

CDC's definition of SV. Appendix A is a glossary of definitions of terms used in this study in relation to college SV.

Prevalence

Prevalence estimates for college SV derive from epidemiological studies, research, and federally mandated data provided by universities. Studies that have yielded estimates of the prevalence of SV on college campuses include the Association of American Universities (AAU) Campus Climate Survey (Cantor et al., 2017, 2020), the Historically Black College and University Campus Sexual Assault Study (Krebs et al., 2011), the Campus Sexual Assault Study (Krebs et al., 2007), Drug-Facilitated, Incapacitated, and Forcible Rape: A National Study (Kilpatrick et al., 2007), the National College Women Sexual Victimization Study (Fisher et al., 2000), and the Koss Scope of Rape Study (Koss et al., 1987, 2022). Each of these studies reported estimates of college SV prevalence using terminology consistent with the CDC's definition of SV.

Koss et al. (1987) were the first to capture the national extent of college SV. They surveyed a sample of 6,159 students at 32 U.S. institutions of higher education and captured data on incidents of sexual aggression and victimization among female participants in two separate time frames: since the age of 14 years and in the 12 months before the survey. Lifetime victimization rates reported by women ranged from 44% (coercion) to 2% (force). Koss et al. (1987) found that one third of women enrolled in college had experienced rape within the 6 months prior to the survey. In a later study, Koss et al. (2022) conducted a longitudinal analysis comparing data sets from 1985 and 2015 to project the current prevalence of rape. The 2015 study involved 2,471 students enrolled in 13 U.S. institutions of higher education. Notable findings included an increase in the reported incidence of victimization through incapacitation from 50% in 1985 to 75% in 2015 and an increase in the reported incidence of rape or attempted rape since the age of 14 years from 27.5% in 1985 to 33% in 2015.

In their longitudinal study, Cantor et al. (2020) found an increase in college SV prevalence during a 5-year period. The researchers conducted the AAU Campus Climate Survey twice, in 2015 and 2019. They distributed the 2015 survey to 21 schools and received 150,072 responses, and they distributed the 2019 survey to 33 schools and received 181,752 responses. The estimated prevalence of self-reported nonconsensual sexual contact involving physical force or inability to consent among undergraduate women in 2019 ranged from 14% to 32% across the 33 schools; despite the substantial variation in prevalence rates, the differences were not statistically significant. Other notable findings reported were as follows: 2019 survey rates were within the range of other surveys using similar criteria to define nonconsensual sexual contact, the estimated prevalence of nonconsensual sexual contact among undergraduate women (25.9%) was 2–3 times higher than that among graduate women and professional students, and the prevalence of nonconsensual sexual contact involving physical force or inability to consent among undergraduate women increased by 3% from 2015 to 2019.

Using a cross-sectional design, Krebs et al. (2007) captured data on the prevalence and effects of sexual assault on college students in their Campus Sexual Assault Study. The researchers used a web-based survey to sample over 6,800 undergraduate students at two large public universities. Their results indicated that 13.7% of participants had been victims of at least one completed sexual assault since entering college. Krebs et al. (2011) reported similar prevalence rates from the Historically Black

College and University Campus Sexual Assault Study, the first to capture SV prevalence on the campuses of historically Black colleges and universities. Using a cross-sectional design and a sample of 3,951 undergraduate students, Krebs et al. (2011) reported that 14% of undergraduate women attending one quarter of historically Black colleges and universities had experienced an attempted (8%) or completed (10%) sexual assault since entering college.

In the National College Women Sexual Victimization Study, Fisher et al. (2000) used a cross-sectional design and sampled 4,446 college women. In this national survey, 15% reported sexual victimization during the year the study was conducted (Fisher et al., 2000). Kilpatrick et al. (2007) conducted another national survey of women in the general and student populations and estimated that 11.5% of women then attending U.S. colleges had been raped. A number of independent researchers have also estimated college SV prevalence rates. Fedina et al. (2018) analyzed 34 independent college SV surveys and data from 84,461 students and found that the prevalence of female sexual victimization was between 6% and 44.2%. Comparing various campus SV prevalence data, Muehlenhard et al. (2017) concluded that one in five undergraduate women had experienced college SV.

The White House Task Force to Protect Students from Sexual Assault (2017) called for colleges to regularly conduct campus climate surveys. These surveys measure the prevalence of SV and the context of SV occurrence. Colleges have received advice on survey design and implementation and sample campus climate surveys. To date, college administrators have determined the content of their campuses' climate surveys, resulting in variations on SV definitions and measurements between campuses and the resulting data (Krause et al., 2018; Swartout et al., 2020).

As a result of these variations, prevalence statistics provided by universities contradict the findings of researchers. The Clery Act required colleges and universities participating in Title IV funding to disclose all campus safety information and publicly outline basic requirements for handling incidents of SV (Palmer & Alda, 2016). Universities submit required data on campus safety to the U.S. Department of Education, which is responsible for publishing university campus safety guidelines and has the authority to audit data and fine noncompliant institutions (Office of Post Secondary Education, 2016). An assumption underlying the Clery Act is that it is possible to obtain reliable and valid statistics.

Risk Factors

Risk factors for college SV victimization are noted across all levels of the SEM (Koss & Dinero, 1989). As conceptualized by the SEM, SV results from multiple interacting levels of influence across the social ecology (DeGue, Valle et al., 2014). The following sections review research studies related to college SV risk factors.

Gender

Gender is a significant factor in college SV. Several research groups have demonstrated that college women are at a greater risk of SV than college men. Cantor et al. (2020) reported that the prevalence of nonconsensual sexual contact involving force or inability to consent was 4 times higher in women than in men. Bhochhibhoya et al. (2021) conducted a cross-sectional study of 361 undergraduate students to identify risk factors for SV among college students in dating relationships. They reported being female as a primary risk factor for sexual victimization, including attempted rape, completed rape, and unwanted sexual contact; the overall prevalence of sexual victimization was approximately five times higher for college women than for college men in their study. Caamano-Isorna et al. (2018) reported similar findings after examining the incidence of sexual and physical assault among university students and its association with alcohol. They found that women were approximately twice as likely as men to experience sexual assault. Wood et al. (2018) studied a diverse sample of students ($N = 17,406$) at eight campuses and analyzed rates of faculty/staff- and peer-perpetrated sexual harassment. Their findings indicated that being female increased the odds of experiencing faculty/staff- and peer-perpetrated sexual harassment by 86% and 147%, respectively; being female also increased the expected rate of experiencing additional peer-perpetrated sexual harassment events by 56%.

Although women as a group are at higher risk than men for college SV, the risk of SV is not the same for all college women (Muehlenhard et al., 2017). Prior sexual victimization, year of college enrollment, differences in campus demographics, and campus culture all are linked to higher risk of SV. For example, strong Greek life or athletic presence and campus cultures that foster binge drinking, hookups, and rape myths are all associated with higher risk of SV (Graham et al., 2014; Marcantonio et al., 2020; Muehlenhard et al., 2017).

Year of Enrollment

Findings from the 2015 AAU Campus Climate Survey, reported by Cantor et al. (2017), indicated that 16.9% of freshman women reported sexual contact by physical force or incapacitation, with only 11.1% of female seniors reporting incidents. Based on the 2019 AAU Campus Climate Survey, Cantor et al. (2020) estimated that the risk of nonconsensual sexual contact by physical force or inability to consent was 2–3 times higher among undergraduate women (25.9%) than among graduate women and professional students. Both study findings suggest that SV prevalence rates decline based on year of enrollment in college.

Data suggest that a woman's risk of SV is greater during the so-called red zone (Cranney, 2015; Flack et al., 2008), the period of time when a woman is first enrolled in college. The exact definition of the red zone varies in the literature from the first semester of a woman's freshman year to the first four semesters (Krebs et al., 2007). Cranney (2015) conducted an exploratory investigation of the red zone using a data set collected in 2005–2011 that included survey results from 22 colleges, including 16,000 female participants. They used a logistic regression and odds ratios to analyze the data and found that, relative to female seniors, female freshmen were 2.014 times more likely to experience physically forced rape and 4.59 times more likely to experience attempted forced rape. These findings confirm that the risk of SV is greater in a woman's freshman year at college. Caamano-Isorna et al. (2018) also identified higher rates of sexual assault during the first 6 months at university.

Alcohol

Researchers have repeatedly identified alcohol use, abuse, and dependence as predictors of college SV (Caamano-Isorna et al., 2018), consequences of college SV (Anderson et al., 2017), and factors negatively influencing a bystander's likelihood of intervening in SV (Marcantonio et al., 2020). Alcohol use has undergone examination both independently and as a variable combined with other risk factors contributing to college SV, such as gender (Caamano-Isorna et al., 2018), hookups (Bhochhibhoya et al., 2021), Greek life (Barnes et al., 2021; Bhochhibhoya et al., 2021; Marcantonio et al., 2020), parties, bars, and social drinking venues (Gilbert et al., 2019), and involvement in sports (Caamano-Isorna et al., 2018).

Caamano-Isorna et al. (2018) studied the incidence of sexual and physical assault and its association with alcohol among 5,170 university students. They conducted their study at three different points in time. The incidence rates of sexual assault for women in their second year at college were 15.1% and 36.4% for those who do not use or depend on alcohol and those who do, respectively. For women in their third year, the corresponding rates were 2.8% and 7.7%. These findings indicate a strong relationship between sexual assault victimization and alcohol in female university students. Barnes et al. (2021) found that of those female participants who experienced nonconsensual sexual contact, 58.6% indicated that at least one event involved coercion or incapacitation via drugs or alcohol.

Ehlke et al. (2019) examined the association between alcohol (quantity and binge drinking), location of consumption (off-campus party or bar/restaurant), and experience of sexual coercion. The study participants ($N = 295$) were female and each self-reported drinking at least once in the 30 days prior to the study. The researchers found that drinking at off-campus parties or bars/restaurants was significantly associated with more drinks per week, which in turn was associated with a greater likelihood of experiencing sexual coercion. Flack et al. (2016) asserted that students who report higher levels of drinking and hooking up are more likely to report sexual assault. They found that the majority of sexual assaults (75%) and attempted or completed rapes (85%) occurred in the context of hooking up.

Greek Life

Martin (2016) described fraternities as *rape prone*, with homogenous membership, hypermasculinity, widespread excessive alcohol use, and social norms that facilitate SV. Fraternities most often control parties and partygoers, providing transportation to parties but not providing safe and reliable transportation back to dorms; coupling this context with their status as private residences outside the jurisdiction of universities increases women's vulnerability.

Lasky et al. (2017) explored the interrelationship between SV victimization involving drugging, Greek life, binge drinking, and non-victimization at three large universities in the South and Midwest. They found that undergraduates who engaged in binge drinking, belonged to Greek sororities, or were first-year students had higher rates of victimization via drugging than their counterparts without those characteristics.

Barnes et al. (2021) examined the risk of sexual assault and harassment associated with sorority and fraternity membership on U.S. college campuses. They recruited participants ($N = 883$) from a large northwestern university. Women in sororities were almost 2 times more likely to report nonconsensual sexual contact, 3 times more likely to report attempted or completed rape, and 2 times more likely to report unwanted sexual attention than non-sorority women. Other researchers have confirmed that women affiliated with sororities frequently experience higher rates of attempted or completed rape than women who are not so affiliated (Canan et al., 2018; Wiersma-Mosley et al., 2017).

Rape Myths

A rape myth is an inaccurate cultural belief that serves to discredit and blame sexual assault victims for their experiences or excuse the behavior of perpetrators, ultimately denying justice to women (Burt, 1980). Rape myths reduce the likelihood of bystanders intervening in incidents of SV (Bannon et al., 2013; McMahon, 2010), provide perpetrators with culturally acceptable excuses for their behavior (O'Neal, 2017), create barriers to holding perpetrators accountable, decrease the likelihood of survivors acknowledging that they have been criminally victimized (Huppin & Malamuth, 2020), increase the likelihood of police officers questioning survivors' credibility (Holland et al., 2021; O'Neal, 2017), and shift responsibility and blame from perpetrators to victims (Canan et al., 2018; O'Neal, 2017).

A review of 105 campus climate surveys showed that only 16% of colleges assessed rape myths (Moylan et al., 2019). In a sample of 524 colleges across the US, Stotzer and MacCartney (2016) found poor institutional support was associated with higher numbers of reports of campus rape. According to Canan et al. (2018), colleges that foster the college experience or campus party culture support rape culture. These researchers found that male students with Greek membership exhibited higher rates of endorsement of rape myth acceptance and token resistance than female students with Greek membership. Women of color who survived college SV perceived that some prevention programming upheld rape myths (Karunaratne & Harris, 2022). College students who hold stronger rape myth attitudes are less likely to intervene in SV incidents (Bannon et al., 2013; McMahon, 2010).

Campus Demographics

Campus demographics associated with risk of SV include whether an institution is public or private, alcohol policies and number of liquor violations, and prevalence of athletes and Greek life (Cranney, 2015; Wiersma-Mosley et al., 2017). Cantor et al. (2020) reported a difference in victimization rates between undergraduate women at the smallest schools in their study (23.9%) and those at the largest schools (27.0%). The percentage of undergraduate women was also positively related to the prevalence of SV among undergraduate women. Schools with the lowest percentages of women had an SV rate of 24.6%, and those with the highest percentages had an SV rate of 27.9%. The schools with the highest percentages of students living on campus had the lowest rate of victimization (23.9%, vs. 26.5% for schools with the lowest percentages of students living on campus).

Using data from the Clery Act, Wiersma-Mosley et al. (2017) examined institutional-level factors that contribute to college SV by comparing campuses with reported rape ($n = 837$) to campuses with no reported rape ($n = 586$). The institutional-level variables they analyzed included tuition, public versus private, percentage of Caucasian students, location, rate of liquor violations, number of fraternity men, athletics, number of athletes, and Division I status. In their analyses they controlled for tuition, public versus private, location, and percentage of Caucasians on campus, which accounted for 12% of the variance for rates of reported rape. Their findings support the belief that systematic differences exist between campuses that report rape and those that do not. When controlling for all other variables, campuses associated with a higher number of rapes were public institutions with higher tuition and more liquor violations, fraternity men, and athletes. The findings did not support geographic location and Division I athletics as factors related to the reporting or rape. However, Stotzer and MacCartney (2016) reported that schools with Division I athletic programs had rates of reported sexual assaults 1.5 times higher than those of schools without athletics programs. Finally, Young et al. (2017) found that, relative to nonathletes, athletes strongly endorsed rape myths; this was true for both intercollegiate and recreational athletes. This finding suggests that rape myth acceptance and traditional gender role attitudes drive athletes to a higher likelihood of sexual coercion. Overall, these findings do not support the claim that all campuses with athletic programs have higher rates of SV, but they do suggest that campus culture and demographics are factors that affect SV incidence.

Prior Victimization

Women who have already experienced SV are at higher risk of revictimization (Cantor et al., 2020; Carey et al., 2015; Fisher et al., 2000; Herres et al., 2018; Mellins et al., 2017). Canan et al. (2018) conducted a secondary analysis of the 2015 AAU Campus Climate Survey, examining the rate of reoccurring victimization among students who had experienced at least one prior episode of SV. Among these students, 69% reported experiencing reoccurring incidents of SV. Results from the National College Women Sexual Victimization Study (Fisher et al., 2000) indicated that of 123 rape victims, 22.8% were victims of multiple rapes.

Mellins et al. (2017) reported findings based on survey data collected from a large, population-based random sample that included undergraduate women ($n = 928$). College women who experienced sexual assault prior to college were 3.01 times more likely to experience penetrative assault and 3.74 times more likely to experience attempted penetrative assault than women who did not experience sexual assault prior to college. The survey data also indicated women faced a cumulative risk of experiencing sexual assault over 4 years of college; by their junior and senior years, respectively, 29.7% and 36.4% of women reported experiencing any sexual assault, compared with 21.0% of freshman women, who had only 1 year of potential exposure. Of women who took the survey as freshmen, 21% had experienced unwanted sexual contact, compared with 36.4% of seniors. This finding supports the conclusions of other researchers that the risk of SV is highest in a college woman's freshman year.

Survivors of college SV are more likely to engage in high-risk behaviors, such as binge drinking and drug use (Fedina et al., 2018), contributing to an even greater risk of revictimization and long-term negative psychological consequences. Prevention of SV on college campuses, effective for general student populations, is ineffective for those who have already been victimized (Mahoney et al., 2020; Vladutiu et al., 2011).

Prevention

The CDC has stressed the importance of primary, secondary, and tertiary SV prevention efforts (Dills et al., 2016) consistent with directives from the White House Task Force to Protect Students from Sexual Assault (2017). An array of college SV prevention programs exist. Some programs include primary and secondary prevention components, and others focus solely on primary prevention. Many SV researchers have studied prevention program components and efficacy. DeGue, Fowler, and Randall (2014) conducted a systematic review of primary prevention program strategies for SV perpetration and examined methodological and programmatic elements of studies published between January 1985 and May 2012. Of 140 studies included in their review, 98 occurred in the college setting. Jouriles et al. (2018) conducted a systematic review and meta-analysis of college SV bystander prevention program delivery methods and outcomes. They included studies published through August 2017 that used a sample of undergraduate students and evaluated a bystander program to reduce SV. The researchers found 24 eligible studies out of 2,458 initial results. Mujal et al. (2019) conducted a systematic review of bystander intervention study characteristics and outcome measures, identifying 44 eligible studies from among 648 published between 2007 and 2017; 75% of the sample were studies of college students.

College SV prevention programs tend to follow one of three models: the bystander model, resistance and risk reduction, and educational programs for men. Despite their different approaches to program delivery, components do overlap between different types of programs. Appendix B provides an overview of available and commonly cited college SV prevention programs and their method of delivery, focus, aims, and underpinnings.

Bystander Model

Latané and Darley (1970) developed the seminal bystander intervention model from their theory of the determinants of responsive bystander behavior. The model includes a series of steps required for intervention in an event: bystanders must notice the event, interpret it as dangerous, take responsibility for intervening, know how to intervene, and choose to act. Banyard et al.'s (2004) application of the bystander model to SV has been impactful. The authors suggested an approach that engages all community members to address SV, shifting from individual and small group centered prevention methods that emphasize rape avoidance and involve criminal justice policies. They further suggested that if community members are not viewed as perpetrators or victims, they will be receptive not only to SV prevention but also to other prosocial behaviors, such as empathy. Empathy is not only important for preventing college SV but also in the aftermath of SV, for supporting survivors.

Central to bystander intervention is the idea that everyone can be an active bystander. Prevention programs rooted in the bystander model aim to reduce the rate of sexual assault and prevent SV by fostering a sense of shared responsibility within a campus community (Senn et al., 2021). Bystander prevention reframes SV as a community issue, ensuring the safety of all community members by empowering them to be active bystanders able to prevent SV by intervening (Banyard et al., 2007). However, significant variation exists in bystander program elements and delivery. Mujal et al. (2019) identified teaching methods in the 44 studies that met their inclusion criteria: presentation was used in 68% of the studies, discussion was used in 54% of the studies, and vignette, active learning skills training, and media all were used in 36% of the studies. Peer educators presented the material in 27% of the studies, school staff in 16%, and web-based presenters and college students in 11%.

Outcome measures for bystander prevention programs, such as Bringing in the Bystander (Banyard et al., 2007), The Men's Project (Gidycz, et al., 2011), and Green Dot (Coker et al., 2019), indicate that these programs increase bystander intentions, bystander actions, and positive attitudes toward bystander behaviors and decrease rape myths. Jouriles et al. (2018) found in their meta-analysis that significant changes from bystander programs continued for up to 3 months following program delivery; however, effects diminished over time. Coker et al. (2017) conducted a 5-year cluster RCT of the ability of a bystander-based program to reduce interpersonal violence. The intervention used in the study was Green Dot, a bystander intervention program. The study outcomes measured were self-reported SV perpetration and victimization. The study sample ($N = 73,795$) consisted of Kentucky high school students from 26 schools. This was the first randomized controlled trial focusing on SV prevention programing implemented with both male and female participants. Victimization rates of SV were 12%–13% lower in the intervention group than in the control group in years 3 and 4 of the study. These findings are not generalizable to college SV; however, they do demonstrate reduced SV in high school populations with bystander intervention.

Bystander intervention programs aim to change rape culture by addressing rape-supportive attitudes and myths. Cadaret et al. (2019) conducted a quasi-experimental study of the efficacy of a bystander prevention program with a strong focus on culture change. The researchers used the Rape Culture Inventory, an 82-item measure, to assess the participants' personal and perceived endorsement of rape culture. The results indicated a sustained decrease in personal and perceived acceptance of rape culture beliefs among intervention participants ($n = 28$) across three time points.

Researchers have identified barriers to bystander intervention. Fischer et al. (2011) found in their meta-analysis of bystander effect literature that bystanders are less likely to intervene if they are in a group; this effect is consistent across different scenarios, including nonemergency situations. Other researchers have supported this finding. Yule and Grych (2017) examined first-year college students' perceptions of barriers to intervening as a bystander. Ninety-three percent of participants reported having encountered a situation where they could have intervened, yet only 27% of participants did intervene in each high-risk situation they encountered. Barriers to intervention identified were *not feeling responsible for doing something* and *not knowing what to do*. These findings suggest that existing bystander programs could be improved by fostering a greater sense of collective responsibility and community in students and teaching specific intervention behaviors. McMahon (2015) reviewed bystander literature and found that sense of community has a strong influence on college students' willingness to intervene as bystanders.

Resistance and Risk Reduction

Sexual violence resistance programs aim to empower female students, teach self-defense, and implement risk reduction strategies by increasing self-protective behaviors (McMahon et al., 2021; Senn et al., 2021). Critics of this method of prevention have asserted that responsibility for reducing risk and stopping SV is placed on the victims (Foubert et al., 2010) and restricts women's lives (Orchowski et al., 2018).

Self-defense classes on university campuses, such as feminist empowerment self-defense, are designed to empower women, increase freedom, and decrease fear (Orchowski et al., 2018). Hollander (2014) used data from a mixed methods study of a 10-week, university-based, feminist self-defense class. A female instructor with 20 years of experience taught the self-defense course. Hollander examined the efficacy of self-defense training over a 1-year period. Participants took the Sexual Experiences Survey and a modified version of the Self-Defense Self-Efficacy Scale at baseline and 1 year later. Hollander (2014) reported increased self-confidence and self-efficacy at the 1-year follow up. Furthermore, women who did not take the class were 1.6 times more likely to experience SV than women who did.

Orchowski et al. (2008) evaluated a modified version of a sexual assault risk reduction and self-defense program. Components of the program included a review of societal factors contributing to SV, a 2-hr feminist self-defense course, and a booster session in which participants reviewed program material. The evaluation included a pretest and 2- and 4-month follow-up assessments. A total of 300 women completed the pretest, of which 137 completed both the 2- and 4-month follow-ups. Self-efficacy increased from pretest ($M = 37.28$, $SD = 7.15$) to the 2-month follow-up ($M = 39.60$, $SD = 5.89$), and gains remained at the 4-month follow-up ($M = 40.65$, $SD = 5.69$). Self-protective behavior levels increased between pretest ($M = 52.15$, $SD = 9.87$) and the 2-month follow-up ($M = 55.13$, $SD = 12.31$), and gains remained at the 4-month follow-up ($M = 55.55$, $SD = 11.96$). Assertive sexual communication increased from the pretest ($M = 125.34$, $SD = 12.91$) to the 4-month follow up ($M = 130.08$, $SD = 12.84$). The quantity and severity of sexual victimization also decreased.

Senn et al. (2017) conducted a RCT in Canada of a sexual assault resistance program. The authors reported secondary and 2-year outcomes of the Enhanced Assess, Acknowledge, Act program, the purpose of which is to help women overcome emotional and cognitive barriers to detecting and acknowledging the increased risk of men's behavior and teach quick and effective resistance strategies (e.g., physical and verbal). Senn et al. (2017) found that the Enhanced Assess, Acknowledge, Act program significantly reduced the incidence of completed rape as early as 6 months after intervention by 58.2%. The intervention efficacy remained for 24-months; at that time point the incidence rate was no longer statistically significant.

Education Programs for Men

Prevention programs developed for male students focus on changing social and gender norms that contribute to SV, such as rape myths and rape culture. Critics of education programs for men have expressed concern about defensive reactions (Katz, 1995). One of the first prevention programs available for men was Mentors in Violence Prevention, which uses a peer leadership model with open discussion and highly interactive trainings to elicit change in attitudes and behaviors (Katz, 1995). Researchers have yet to confirm its effects of behavior with formal rigorous testing (Orchowski et al., 2018).

The Men's Project is a prevention program that incorporates social norms and bystander intervention techniques and is implemented with men. Gidycz et al. (2011) conducted a study of the effects of the Men's Project on college men's self-reported sexual aggression. Participants ($N = 635$) underwent assessment prior to the program and at 4- and 7-month follow-ups. Participants reported less reinforcement for engaging in sexually aggressive behavior, fewer associations with sexually aggressive peers, and less exposure to sexually explicit media after the program. Participants did not indicate a higher likelihood of intervening as a bystander after the program.

Salazar et al. (2018) conducted a randomized controlled trial of RealConsent components and theoretical mediators. RealConsent is a web-based SV prevention program that addresses both SV perpetration and prosocial bystander behaviors. Salazar et al. measured outcomes (e.g., reduction in sexual coercion perpetration and increase in prosocial intervening) at the completion of the intervention and at a 6-month follow-up. At the 6-month follow-up, participants in the intervention group ($n = 215$) reported less SV and more intervening prosocial behaviors. However, the follow-up had a high attrition rate, a limitation of the study.

Findings reported in existing literature support a variety of college SV prevention program components and delivery methods. However, they do not support prevention programs' long-term efficacy or ability to reduce college SV (McMahon et al., 2021). Furthermore, researchers have not demonstrated a relationship between prevention program attendance and reduction in SV prevalence; nor have they extensively explored survivors' attitudes and experiences toward SV prevention programs (DeGue, Valle et al., 2014). The individual and social costs of college SV are significant. It is thus necessary to continue efforts to understand how to prevent college SV.

Disclosure

Survivors of college SV disclose their experiences infrequently. Halstead et al. (2017) conducted a systematic review and found that 25%–55% of college women did not disclose their SV experiences to anyone. Koss et al. (1987) reported similar findings, asserting that 42% of rape survivors never disclosed their rapes. Moylan et al. (2019) reviewed 105 campus climate surveys and found that more than a quarter of survivors did not formally or informally report their experiences.

Cantor et al. (2020) reported that 85.9% of college women told at least one other person, most commonly a friend (81.9%), followed by a close family member. Many researchers have reported that college women often disclose instances of SV informally, such as to friends, roommates, or family members (Franklin & Garza, 2021; Hassija &

Turchik, 2016; Orchowski & Gidycz, 2012). Sabina and Ho (2014) reviewed 45 SV studies and found that women's close female friends and (less frequently) family members were the primary recipients of informal disclosures of college SV. The authors also found that benefits of informal disclosure, such as positive social support, were discussed in each of the 45 studies, and negative reactions to informal disclosure were reported infrequently.

Barriers

Many authors have discussed barriers to informal and formal reporting. Orchowski and Gidycz (2012) reported that the rate of informal disclosure decreased as the level of acquaintance with the perpetrator increased; survivors who had previously experienced SV were also less likely than others to disclose, either formally or informally. According to Sabri et al. (2019), survivors of SV reported benefits of having access to peers' stories, which helped them to better understand how their disclosure would play out before they disclosed their experiences. In a study of 42 SV survivors, S. E. Ullman et al. (2020) found that nondisclosure or selective disclosure may benefit survivors by allowing them to avoid harmful reactions and revictimization.

Formal Disclosure

Sabina and Ho's (2014) examination of 45 empirical studies revealed that college sexual assault victims reported to police 0%–12.9% of the time. Spencer et al. (2017) confirmed that 95% of sexual assault survivors do not report their assault to university officials. Kilpatrick et al. (2007) determined that approximately 12% of rapes of college women are reported to law enforcement. In their longitudinal study, Cantor et al. (2017, 2020) found no change over 4 years in the percentage of victimized students who did not report to campus officials or law enforcement, despite expansion of formal supports on college campuses.

Fear of not being believed and expectation of lack of support are barriers to reporting SV incidents to university officials or law enforcement (Holland, 2020; Sabri et al., 2019). According to Schulze and Budd (2020), universities with aggressive and visible SV policies and those that publicly recognize the prevalence of sexual assault are the most likely to provide supportive environments that encourage formal disclosure by survivors. Spencer et al. (2017) described similar findings: survivors reported that they were more likely to formally report an assault to university officials if they had a general positive perception of the overall campus climate.

Sabri et al. (2019) conducted a qualitative study of college SV survivors' perspectives on barriers to disclosure. Participants overwhelmingly reported feeling that nothing positive would result from reporting the incident to the university authorities or police. Factors identified as barriers to reporting included the university's climate, fear of not being believed, use of alcohol, loss of control, and the lengthy reporting process. Several survivors expressed concern about the negative social impact of reporting and emphasized the importance of campus support resources for maintaining survivor anonymity and confidentiality. Participants in Spencer et al.'s (2017) study also emphasized the importance of confidentiality and felt that regulations safeguarding survivors' privacy and preventing disclosure of their names and addresses would be either moderately (34.4%) or highly (61.5%) beneficial in improving their willingness to report instances of SV to authorities.

Lindquist et al. (2016) conducted a cross-sectional study of the sexual assault disclosure experiences of women attending historically Black colleges and universities. In a web-based survey with both open- and closed-ended questions, college SV survivors ($n = 438$) reported that they disclosed to someone close to them (e.g., family or friends; $n = 238$); to a victim, crisis, or health care center ($n = 39$); or to law enforcement ($n = 24$). Survivors reported not wanting anyone to know, fear of reprisal, and embarrassment as the most common reasons for not reporting to victim crisis centers, health centers, or law enforcement. Of the total sample, 70% ($n = 2{,}782$) answered open-ended questions that resulted in 14 main themes summarizing strategies that would increase sexual assault reporting to law enforcement. The most common strategies recommended were increasing sexual assault awareness, raising awareness of existing services for survivors, enhanced/accessible services, providing anonymous reporting options, and maintaining confidentiality. Lowenstein-Barkai (2020) described disclosure to online support groups or social media accounts as an overall safe and supportive environment, "which even enjoys some affordances that lack from offline settings, and hence holds advantageous potential effects for their psychological and physical health outcomes" (p. 24).

Alcohol is a substantial risk factor for college SV, but authors have also frequently described alcohol as a barrier to formal disclosure, attributable to fear of breaching campus policies or being blamed for drinking. Cantor et al. (2020) reported that 54% of women who reported SV experiences involving penetration did not contact a program or resource because alcohol was involved. Sabina and Ho (2014) found that substance use by perpetrator and victim before an SV incident was positively associated with informal disclosure and negatively associated with formal disclosure.

Using a vignette-based, between-subjects factorial design, Henry et al. (2022) examined the different ways intoxication levels impact perceptions of campus sexual assault. The researchers provided the participants ($N = 276$) with a campus assault vignette to read and then asked them to complete a questionnaire that measured their perceptions of the people involved. Contrary to prior research on the impact of alcohol on perceptions of blame, the participants blamed victims less and more strongly considered an incident to be rape or sexual assault when victims were highly intoxicated. The authors noted that there were several high-profile SV cases in the US during the study, combined with increased SV activism (e.g., *Me Too*, Time's Up). The authors reported that their findings may have been influenced by shifting attitudes around SV or the heightened national awareness of SV.

Disclosure is intertwined with many factors surrounding college SV such as alcohol, rape myths, and campus support. The usefulness of official reports, such as Clery Act data, is limited by low rates of disclosure to campus officials or community law enforcement. Linking survivors to campus support services necessitates disclosure by those survivors of their SV experiences. Lack of disclosure complicates the identification of college SV risk factors and the development of trauma-informed prevention and intervention programs.

Support

The response and social support college women receive after disclosure of SV has a lasting effect on their overall health and well-being. Researchers have classified social reactions to survivors of SV following disclosure of SV incidents as negative (non-supportive) or positive (supportive). Supportive reactions to SV disclosure express emotional (e.g., listening and comforting) and informational support, tangible aid, or a sense of belonging. Positive social reactions from formal and informal support increase self-worth and improve psychological outcomes, such as by reducing anxiety and depression. In contrast, unsupportive reactions include blaming the victim, expressing doubt, or withdrawing from relationships. Negative reactions to survivor disclosure may worsen the psychological influence of the incident (Ahrens et al., 2010). Survivors' insight into, and experience with, social support following the disclosure of college SV provides applicable information on helpful aspects, existing barriers, and the support necessary for survivors in the aftermath of an assault to alleviate negative psychological and physical trauma associated with SV.

Informal

The intention guiding the design of intervention programs such as Supporting Survivors and Self was education of individuals who may be sources of informal support to survivors. The aim of the program is to improve supportive responses when a survivor discloses an incident of SV (Edwards, Waterman et al., 2020). Program components are designed to encourage victim empathy and diminish victim blame. Edwards, Ullman et al. (2020) studied a secondary outcome data set from a randomized controlled trial measuring the effect of Supporting Survivors and Self on depression symptoms secondary to SV. Six months after participants completed Supporting Survivors and Self, the authors sent participants a survey. Participants who reported one form of SV in the six months prior to the survey were included in the secondary outcome study ($n = 187$). Their results suggest that interventions designed to provide informal support to survivors can effectively reduce psychological distress in those who are subsequently victimized.

Informal support has significantly expanded over the last decade to include online support. Mendes et al. (2018) conducted a case study of digital feminist activism to raise feminist consciousness and generate solidarity. The data set in the case study derived from multiple sources and included #BeenRapedNeverReported tweets and interviews with women who used the hashtag to share online their experiences of SV. Participants reported receiving significant support after tweeting about their assaults. One participant who had experienced college SV said that sharing her experience online provided her with the strength to report her assault to the campus police. In addition, Lowenstein-Barkai (2020) examined support for SV survivors who disclosed their status online. Ninety-eight percent of responses were supportive and included different expressions of support, such as "I believe you," "It is so frustrating!" "You are amazing," and "I'm by your side."

Formal

Survivors may receive support from service providers at their institutions through Title IX offices, counseling and health service centers, and faculty. Moreover, several campuses have established sexual assault centers and victim advocacy services to support survivors after assaults (Holland, 2020). Institutions that can provide comprehensive trauma-informed services may partner with community-based organizations, such as rape crisis centers (Reingold & Gostin, 2015). Additional community support providers and services may be available through local law enforcement agencies, sexual assault nurse examiners, and hospitals. On most campuses, college health centers (CHCs) are available for survivors.

However, not all CHCs offer post-assault aftercare. Furthermore, the availability of sexual assault nurse examiners has been limited both on campus and in the community where the campus is situated. During the 2017–2018 academic year, only 10 (6%) of 171 schools surveyed offered post-assault care with a sexual assault nurse examiner (ACHA, 2020). The primary function of formal support resources is to support survivors' recovery; however, survivors have used them less often than they have used informal support (R. Campbell et al., 2008; Sabina & Ho, 2014). Researchers have identified various reasons survivors do not seek formal support in the aftermath of an incident, including the belief that the incident is not that serious (Edwards, Ullman et al., 2020), lack of awareness and accessibility of campus services (McMahon et al., 2018; Mitra et al., 2021), mandatory reporting policies (Holland et al., 2021), and lack of confidentiality (Mitra et al., 2021; Sabri et al., 2019).

Mitra et al. (2021) conducted a qualitative study using in-depth interviews and focus group discussions to identify barriers to students accessing Campus Assault Resources and Education offices on three University of California campuses. Faculty, graduates, and undergraduate students ($n = 68$ in interviews, and $n = 27$ in focus groups) participated in the study as well as community stakeholders. The focus of the study extended beyond survivors' experiences, but survivors were among the participants and provided insight into their experiences. The following themes emerged as barriers to, and facilitators of, accessing Campus Assault Resources and Education offices: (a) awareness of the offices, (b) confidentiality of services, (c) physical accessibility, (d) accessibility for vulnerable and marginalized groups, (e) utilization experiences, and (f) limited institutional support.

Holland and Cortina (2017) conducted a qualitative study of why survivors did not use three formal campus support options: the Title IX office, the sexual assault center, and housing staff (resident assistants) for post-assault care. Every participant ($N = 284$) had experienced at least one form of SV as a student and was a woman. However, only 5.6% of the participants reported that they had disclosed SV to one of the three campus support options available. The other participants described their reasons for not disclosing to one of these support resources as lack of knowledge about what help the support resource could provide, involvement of alcohol, not wanting to disclose the incident to a mandated reporter and wanting to forget the incident happened.

Campus resident assistants (RAs) are uniquely positioned among formal supports for survivors of college SV because RAs are peers of the survivors. Over the past decade federal mandates and institutional policies have positioned RAs as campus security authorities and mandated reporters. To understand how RAs respond to the disclosure of SV and the implications of these responses, Holland and Bedera (2019) studied 305 RA responses to student sexual assault disclosure scenarios through critical discourse analysis. The researchers identified four discourses used by RAs when communicating about resources to hypothetical sexual assault victims: controlling, gatekeeping, minimizing, and empowering. Controlling responses (45%) were the most common and included statements on what a survivor should or must do following an assault. Minimizing responses (20%) were the second most common and included responses expressing a low degree of certainty that a survivor needed resources but communicating that the survivor could access resources if they *really needed* them.

Through critical discourse analysis, Holland and Cipriano (2020) explored how RAs engage with the concept of consent in SV disclosure. They identified both supportive and unsupportive responses. Supportive responses by the RAs identified the right to deny unwanted sex and included language that reflected the university's sexual misconduct policy. Unsupportive responses came from RAs who had difficulty identifying coercion as indicating lack of consent and said a survivor should have acted differently in their situation. Holland et al. (2021) examined the role of rape myths and feminism on the likelihood of RAs referring survivors to sexual assault centers. The researchers found that RAs who were more accepting of rape myths were less likely to provide emotional support and refer survivors to sexual assault centers. When agents of formal support services question survivors, blame them for the assaults they have experienced, or fail to assist them, survivors are left to question the usefulness and purpose of seeking out such services.

Halstead et al. (2018) explored female undergraduates' perspectives on the role of a CHC as a resource for SV in a qualitative descriptive study. The researchers relied on a convenience sample of undergraduate university students. They conducted four focus groups using an 11-question focus group guide. Three major themes emerged: support and barriers to using the CHC for SV, the CHC's responsibility to educate students about SV, and the CHC's responsibility to implement comprehensive campus-wide SV efforts. The center's location was both a support and a barrier. Participants indicated that it would be easier to seek help or disclose SV incidents on campus. Although some students found the on-campus location convenient, for those without transportation, confidentiality concerns and limited hours were barriers to use. However, several expressed limited knowledge of what services the center offered. Solutions described by participants included education on the CHC's role in SV via pamphlets and flyers and routine SV screening.

Eisenberg et al. (2016) conducted a quantitative study of associations between resources on college campuses for SV prevention and intervention and the mental health of students who experienced SV. The researchers gathered the number of resources (e.g., hotline/24-hr support, safe walking escort services, SV awareness activities, SV support group counseling, and SV pamphlets/posters) available on 28 campuses. Participants ($N = 326$) answered questions about any new diagnoses for anxiety, depression, panic attacks, and PTSD and their overall emotional well-being over the previous year. Rates of diagnosed mental health conditions among the participants ranged from 6.4% for PTSD to 19.8% for anxiety. Women at colleges with low SV resources had PTSD at a rate 4 times that of women at colleges with high resources. Eisenberg et al.'s findings suggest that undergraduate survivors attending campuses with more survivor support resources have fewer mental health conditions than those attending campuses with fewer resources. The researchers did not describe the specific campus resources chosen by survivors.

Know Your IX (2021), an SV activist group, surveyed 100 survivors and reported that 100% of those surveyed received negative treatment (e.g., victim-blaming, name-calling, stalling of cases, or being informed that the school could not help them) from their institution's Title IX offices. Fleming et al. (2018) found survivors rated Title IX coordinators and university officials "unhelpful." Their sample consisted of 217 undergraduate student survivors, 89% of whom were female. Further, Holland and Cipriano (2021) conducted a qualitative study to explore survivors' perceptions of, and interactions with, their institution's Title IX office. Four overarching themes emerged related to the study participants' ($N = 7$) experiences with their institution's Title IX office: lack of action against the perpetrator, inconsistency, lack of transparency, and mistreatment (e.g., lack of empathy and survivors being told officials were not there to advocate or be supportive). Although Title IX offices are locations for institutional support, the evidence reported in existing literature suggests that survivors do not find these offices supportive.

Gómez (2021) used campus climate survey data to characterize college SV, cultural betrayal, and institutional responses by gender in college students belonging to minority ethnic groups. They used the Institutional Betrayal and Support Questionnaire to assess institutionally supportive behaviors. Institutional betrayal can be isolated or systemic and is related to action or inaction by an institution. Because the questionnaire's assessment of institutional treatment relates to victimization, only participants who disclosed any victimization ($n = 63$) completed it. The researchers found that 90% of participants who had been victimized reported institutional betrayal (97.7% of college women and 80.0% of college men). Internal consistency of the Institutional Betrayal and Support Questionnaire was excellent for both institutional betrayal ($\alpha = .97$) and institutional support ($\alpha = .97$). The authors suggested that institutions solicit anonymous feedback from students who access campus resources to improve isolated and systemic behaviors and create a more supportive campus environment. Edwards, Waterman et al. (2020) noted that negative social support following survivors' disclosure could result in self-blame, increasing the likelihood of negative psychological outcomes, such as PTSD, anxiety, and depression. Strong social support reduces the likelihood of revictimization and is the strongest protective factor against PTSD (Eisenberg et al., 2016; Hawn et al., 2018).

Consequences

Researchers have thoroughly documented the negative impacts of college SV on women's physical and psychological health. Survivors of SV experience immediate and long-term consequences that impact their relationships, education, and career aspirations.

Physical

Cantor et al. (2020) found that 15.1% of women who had experienced SV reported physical injuries from penetration, and 4.6% reported contracting a sexually transmitted disease. Amar and Gennaro (2005) conducted a quantitative study of the types of violence occurring in the dating experiences of college women that resulted in physical injuries and the need for subsequent health care. The researchers used the Abuse Assessment Screen to measure the occurrence of interpersonal violence among the participants ($n = 412$). They provided a list of physical injuries consistent with existing literature on interpersonal violence and the National Violence Against Women Survey. Of the participants who reported physical injuries ($n = 132$)—such as bruises, black eyes, genital injuries, sprains, strains, and sexually transmitted disease—40% sought health care, most commonly through an outpatient appointment with a health care provider ($n = 27$), student health services ($n = 18$), or emergency services ($n = 18$).

Psychological

Dworkin et al. (2017) conducted a review and meta-analysis of sexual assault victimization and psychopathy and found that sexual assault was associated with an increased risk of all forms of psychopathology, PTSD, suicidal ideation, and attempting suicide. Their analysis, although not specific to college SV, demonstrates the mental health risks associated with SV for survivors. Eisenberg et al. (2016) found that college SV survivors ($n = 326$) reported an average of 11.0 days during the previous month when their emotional health was poor and 6.2 days when their poor mental health interfered with regular activities. Self-reported rates of diagnosis of mental health conditions among survivors ranged from 6.4% for PTSD to 19.8% for anxiety; Herres et al. (2018) reported similar findings. Applying the SEM to examine correlates of college SV and moderators of risk across ecological systems, Herres et al. (2018) found that 11.2% of participants reported experiencing clinically significant levels of PTSD symptoms. The symptoms were also associated with reduced awareness of campus services and with poorer perceptions of the campus community, student supportiveness, the college's responsiveness to reports of college SV, and the college's handling of college SV.

Cantor et al. (2020) reported that female SV survivors experienced other consequences affecting their well-being, such as loss of interest in daily activities (40.9%), withdrawal from interactions with friends (46.4%), nightmares or trouble sleeping (42.2%), and feeling numb or detached (60.2%). Claydon et al. (2022) investigated the association between exposure to interpersonal violence and sexual assault and clinically significant eating disorder symptomology in college students. The authors reported that college women who experienced interpersonal violence or sexual assault were 2.68 times more likely to experience clinically significant eating disorder symptomology than college women who experienced neither.

Academic and Career

Potter et al. (2018) studied undergraduate SV survivors to examine their mental and physical health problems and explore how trauma impacted their lifetime education trajectories and career attainment. Through Qualtrics surveys and phone interviews, the researchers included a total of 81 women. Of those, 72.8% reported that their mental health complications were absent prior to their trauma, and 71.6% reported coping with mental health problems that affected their academic endeavors. Brewer et al. (2018) similarly found that interpersonal violence was associated with poor academic performance as a result of psychological distress.

Banyard et al. (2017) sampled 6,482 undergraduate students (2,207 men and 4,275 women) to measure the relationship between academic outcomes and experiences of SV, intimate partner violence, and stalking victimization. Using Pearson's correlations and multivariate analysis of variance, the researchers compared self-reported academic outcomes (academic efficacy, collegiate stress, institutional commitment, and scholastic conscientiousness) with the impact of victimization for four types of victimization (interpersonal violence, unwanted sexual contact, unwanted sexual intercourse, and stalking). They found significant main effects across the four academic outcomes for three of the four types of victimization: interpersonal violence, unwanted intercourse, and stalking. The main effect for unwanted sexual contact was not significant.

Cantor et al. (2020) reported the results of 33 campus climate surveys administered to member schools of the AAU and analyzed the effects of SV on education. Although the purpose of the AAU campus climate surveys was to address concerns related to the incidence and prevalence of sexual assault and misconduct

(Cantor et al., 2017), the responses offered information on the academic and professional consequences of SV. Sixty-two percent of women reported at least one academic or professional consequence; the most common was difficulty concentrating on studies, assignments, and exams (55.5%); this was followed by decreased class attendance (36.3%) and decreased work attendance (23.3%). Patterson Silver Wolf et al. (2016) examined data from the National College Health Survey and reported that Indigenous undergraduate women who had been sexually assaulted or raped during their freshman years ended those years with significantly lower grade point averages than those who had not been assaulted.

Activism

Sexual violence activism significantly increased in the 1970s, coinciding with the Women's Movement, led by feminists and community organizers (Driessen, 2020). During this period, student activists successfully campaigned for the first campus rape crisis center (Driessen, 2020). Organizers also held the first Take Back the Night rally, now an annual event on college campuses that brings awareness to SV and allows SV survivors to share their experiences. Survivors of SV often turn to anti-sexual assault activism to cope with and heal their trauma (Strauss Swanson & Szymanski, 2020).

Scoglio et al. (2021) conducted a qualitative study of SV responders to explore the perspectives of the survivors the responders work with regarding pathways to healing and justice. The theme of involvement in activism surfaced in their analysis. Participants discussed how engaging in activism was a component of healing for the survivors with whom they worked. Based on the responders' experiences, activism is both healing and triggering. However, survivors who found support in their communities wanted to give back to them. Participants discussed how changes in the social climate had impacted their work and the healing of survivors they worked with. Participants mentioned the positive influence of the Me Too movement multiple times.

The Me Too movement, founded by SV survivor and activist Tarana Burke in 2006, went viral with the hashtag #MeToo in 2017. Hollywood actress Alyssa Milano popularized the term by posting it to Twitter in response to a report in the *New York Times* of sexual assault by Harvey Weinstein. Since the initial post by Milano in 2017 through September 2021 the #MeToo hashtag was used over 19 million times on Twitter (Anderson & Toor, 2018). The Me Too movement contributed to an increase in SV reporting (Williamson et al., 2020), provided awareness of the types of violence experienced by survivors, and offered insights into survivors' reasons for not reporting their experiences (Guidry et al., 2021). Over the past decade, student activists and SV survivors on college campuses have used technological advances to amplify their voices and connect with one another in response to the handling of SV by institutions; they have also used these advances to promote cultural change and elevate the issue to the national policy agenda (Bovill et al., 2021; Gronert, 2019; Marine & Trebisacci, 2018). Social media platforms (e.g., Facebook, Instagram, and Twitter) have allowed SV survivors to share their stories and connect with others who have experienced similar trauma.

Social media sites such as Instagram and Twitter have increasingly become a forum for survivor disclosure, raising of awareness, and responding to SV (Bogen et al., 2019; Guidry et al., 2021). For example, researchers assessing content on Instagram and Twitter that contains hashtags such as #NotOkay (Guidry et al., 2021; Maas et al., 2018), #MaybeHeDoesntHitYou (McCauley et al., 2018), #WhyILeft, and #WhyIStayed

(Weathers et al., 2016) have found that some social media users post SV experiences and others provide support to survivors, raising overall awareness of the pervasiveness of SV. Callender and Klassen (2020) assessed how college women experienced the Me Too movement and found that participants felt the movement was a supportive force in society, a safe place for connecting with others who have survived SV, and a catalyst for encouraging others to seek help following SV. Additionally, participants reported that interacting with the Me Too movement made them feel empowered; engaging in advocacy for themselves and showing solidarity with other survivors was an essential component of their recovery.

Summary

This literature review provides a comprehensive overview of the current research related to the study. A substantial body of research exists on college SV. Studies show the prevalence of college SV remains high, is underreported, women are disproportionately affected, and has not improved in 30 years (Moylan et al., 2019). Prevention program strategies are aimed at known risk factors and target various audiences. The literature suggests the bystander approach to prevention positively impacts attitudes and social norms, short-term. Risk reduction and male education prevention programs have had varying reported outcomes in SV prevention. Existing evidence does not support the premise that college SV prevention programs decrease the rates of SV on college campuses.

The literature demonstrates that college SV survivors often want their voices to be heard. Women survivors have turned to activism for self-healing, and to encourage and support other survivors. Yet, few SV researchers have elicited female survivors' experiences of college SV. Beyond evaluating college students' attitudes and beliefs, studies are needed to understand the multiple levels of interaction where college SV occurs.

Chapter 3: Methodology

Chapter Three presents the qualitative methodology used for this study. This chapter details the study design, the setting for the study, and protection of human rights. Next, data collection and the study sample are presented followed by data analysis plan, trustworthiness, and rigor.

Study Design

A qualitative descriptive approach was used to examine college women's experiences of SV. The qualitative descriptive method emphasizes the characteristics of phenomena as presented by a study's participants (Sandelowski, 2000). The origins of the qualitative descriptive method lie in the social sciences, and its philosophical assumptions are naturalistic (Bradshaw et al., 2017). Researchers conducting qualitative descriptive research seek to understand a phenomenon, a process, or the perspectives of participants (Caelli et al., 2003) and provide rich descriptions of experiences in straightforward language (Bradshaw et al., 2017).

Using a qualitative descriptive method, guided by the SEM, resulted in a straightforward and comprehensive summary (Bradshaw et al., 2017) of college SV in the language of female survivors. Framing the study within the SEM allowed for examination of multiple levels of influence in relation to college SV. Quantitative research encompasses the study of research questions and hypotheses that describe phenomena, test relationships, and seek to explain cause and effect among variables, but qualitative research rests on the assumption that researchers can only understand phenomena if they consider the context in which those phenomena take place.

The purpose of this study was not to redescribe the experiences of female college SV survivors, establish causal relationships among variables, or compare groups. Rather, the study's purpose was to examine survivors' experiences within the SEM to provide an in-depth understanding of college SV as described by female survivors. This method was chosen because its objectives are congruent with the study research questions.

Setting

The setting for the study is a public university in the northeastern US with approximately 14,000 undergraduate students. Social media platforms (e.g., Twitter, Facebook, and Instagram) are designed for communication by and among readers. Seventy percent of adults used social media, and 71% of 18–29-year-olds used Instagram (Pew Research Center, 2021). Instagram is primarily a photo sharing social media site that was first launched in October 2010 (Instagram.com). One or more SV activists attending the university created an account in June 2020 on Instagram. The first post on the account was created on June 27, 2020, and the last post was created on December 22, 2021; 891 posts were used and present on the account at the start of this study. The activist(s) who created the Instagram account have identified as SV survivor(s) and describe the purpose of the Instagram site as providing an anonymous and confidential platform for SV survivors at their university to disclose their experiences with SV. Survivors who wish to share their experiences can do so through a link on the Instagram page that directs them to a Google Form. The form provides further information on submitting stories, and SV survivors can create a password corresponding to their personal story to facilitate editing or removal of the story.

Human Subjects Protection

This study underwent the review and approval process managed by the Binghamton University Institutional Review Board (IRB). The study met the criteria for exempt status, therefore was categorized as exempt (Appendix C). The data are publicly available on a social media site, Instagram. Names of survivors who have shared their stories are absent from the Instagram account, and the names of the account moderators are not known. According to Moreno et al. (2013), if access to a social media site is public, if information is identifiable but not private, and if there is no interaction with the individual who has posted it online, then it may be presumed that a project using the information does not constitute human subject research. Nevertheless, all data for this study, including survivor stories, memos, a reflective journal, and an audit trail, were kept on a password-protected computer.

Data Collection

Data collection in qualitative descriptive studies focuses on the who, what, and where of events or experiences or on their basic nature and shape (Neergaard et al., 2009; Sandelowski, 2000). Gathering information in an individual's natural setting emphasizes the role of the researcher as an active learner (Sandelowski, 2000) conveying the stories of participants rather than as an expert in their experiences. In extracting the data from the social media site, the chronological order in which posts appeared online was maintained, and posts were numbered as such (e.g., "1/4" and "1/5") and uploaded into the qualitative data analysis software application MAXQDA as described in the Data Sample and Data Analysis sections.

Data Sample

A purposeful sampling strategy, maximum variation, was used to identify essential and variable features of SV as described by survivors for the study. Purposive sampling involves selecting a sample based on a specific purpose (Teddlie & Yu, 2007). Maximum variation is a purposeful sampling technique useful for obtaining broad insights and rich information and identifying and expanding the range of variation or differences (Neergaard et al., 2009; Palinkas et al., 2015; Sandelowski, 2000). Maximum variation sampling is appropriate for selecting stories told by survivors of SV for the study because it allowed for a breadth of perspectives rather than limiting the sample to representation of survivor stories specific to the prevention of, or intervention in, SV.

Study data were 891 posts on a single Instagram account. Posts on the account include information from moderators and survivor experiences. The survivors who shared their experiences are individuals who identify as men or women, and lesbian, gay, bisexual, transgender, or queer/questioning. Survivors detailed their experiences of SV and the aftermath in as little as three sentences and as many as two paragraphs. Women's stories included in the study were those that occurred during enrollment in the university and include experiences of college SV. In this study the term *story* is used. A *story* is a de facto disclosure which a survivor has chosen to share in an unscripted way. The use of the word *story* on social media comes from the language of the Me Too movement in which women and others have shared their experiences of SV (McCue et al., 2021). The term *story* in this study represents survivors' experiences of college SV and the meaning they assign to it.

Limited demographic information (e.g., gender, race, and age) was available in the data from the Instagram platform. Each story was read in its entirety. Stories in which female gender could be inferred (based on contextual details) and the SV experience(s) occurred while enrolled in the university were uploaded into a separate file on MAXQDA. Only stories where gender inference was possible were included. Stories that did not describe college SV experiences or described SV that occurred before enrollment in the university were also excluded. During the data analysis process, described in the following section, each story was read and checked for sampling errors. Those stories that occurred during enrollment in the university and described women's experiences of SV were included.

Data Analysis

Women's SV experiences were analyzed in an iterative five-cycle inductive and deductive process described by Bingham and Witkowsky (2022), (see Figure 2). The deductive analysis allowed for the application of the SEM, the organization of the data, and the maintenance of focus on the research questions (Miles et al., 2019). The inductive approach allowed for emerging topics and themes within the data (Miles et al., 2019). Throughout the analysis process, memos were written to capture emerging ideas and relationships, explore and summarize the data, explicate PI positionality, and thoughts on further research. During cycle three and four of the analysis process a code book was drafted which contains each code, a brief definition, and a description. Throughout the analysis process, example quotes were added to the code book.

Cycle one and two are deductive strategies used in the analysis process. First, the study data of 891 posts were read several times to gain an overall impression of the content and to begin to organize the date. While reviewing the data, attribute codes were applied to begin sorting the data into organizational categories (i.e., survivor stories, moderator posts). Attribute coding records essential information regarding the data and demographic characteristics of the participants for management and reference (Saldana, 2021). At the end of cycle one the data that met inclusion criteria, 384 college women's stories of college SV, were placed in a separate file in MAXQDA for further analysis. The final study sample (n = 384) includes 384 women's stories of college SV. Next, each survivor story was carefully read to align it to a category related to the research questions. The second cycle of the analysis process was not straightforward as it became clear several of the survivors' stories contained categories within the SEM that were overlapping. To maintain focus during this cycle, key concepts from the SEM were reviewed and compared to the college women's stories to identify the most relevant potential influences at each level of the model.

Cycles three and four followed inductive data analysis strategies. In cycle three of the analysis, the stories were read multiple times and the process of open coding began to identify the concepts and phenomena of the study. Cycle four of the analytic process involves patterned coding and produced the study findings. Patterned coding is the process of grouping the codes into a smaller number of categories, themes, or concepts (Miles et al., 2019).

Finally, cycle five followed both deductive and inductive analytic strategies. In cycle five of the analysis the conceptual model was applied to the study findings. This cycle produced an explanation of the study findings based on the SEM. In addition, during this cycle the study findings were situated in the literature to identify explanations for the themes.

Figure 2

Five-cycle Data Analysis

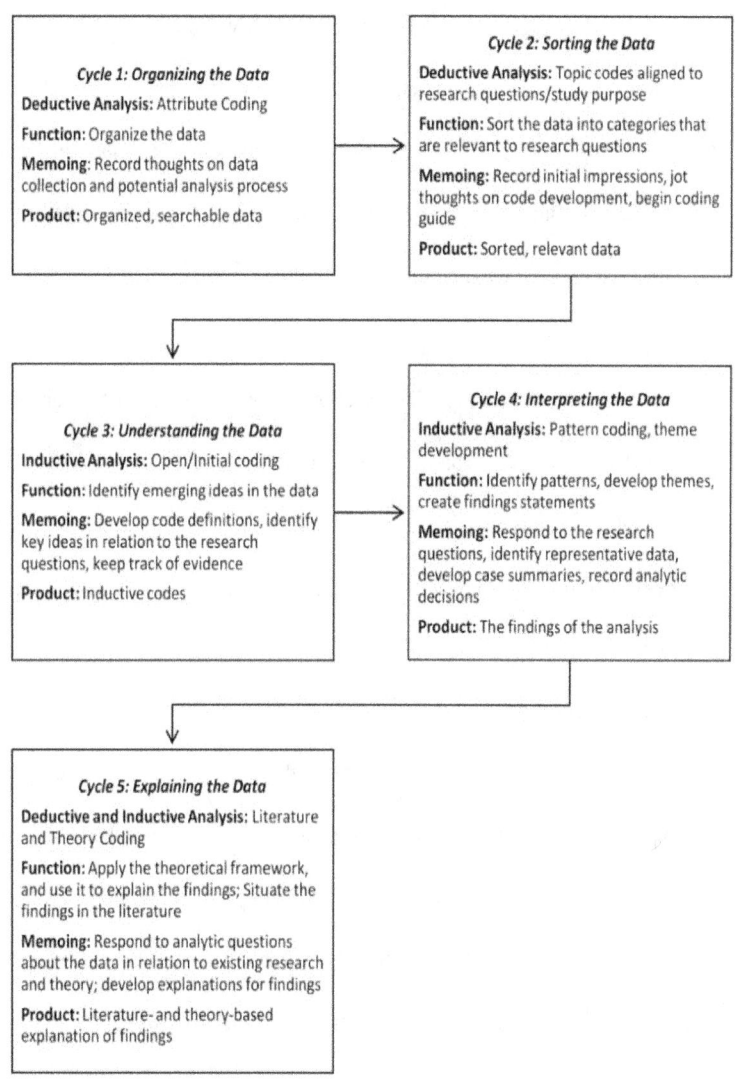

Note: See Bingham & Witkowsky, (2022)

Rigor and Trustworthiness

Historically, qualitative studies have been criticized for their for their lack of rigor (Neergaard et al., 2009) therefore, Creswell and Poth (2017) recommend using established criteria to help ensure trustworthy and rigorous qualitative findings. Lincoln and Guba (1985) developed a framework to ensure trustworthiness that qualitative researchers can follow. Their framework, which was used in this study, includes four criteria: credibility, dependability, confirmability, and transferability. These criteria intended to respond to four aspects of trustworthiness: truth value, applicability, consistency, and neutrality (Lincoln & Guba, 1985). The sections that follow address how each measure was applied in the study to achieve rigor and trustworthiness.

Credibility

Analytic memoing is the creation of brief narratives that include thoughts and reflections during data collection and analysis (Miles et al., 2019). The analytic memos created during the study offer transparency in the process. Additionally, direct quotes were taken from the data to maintain the true nature of the data and improve the credibility of the themes.

Dependability

Creating an audit trail ensures that the findings of the study are reproducible if the inquiry occurred with the same participants. The audit trail contains detailed descriptions of procedures implemented throughout the study along with rationales for decisions made. The study code book enables the possibility of replication, adding to the rigor of the study (Roberts et al., 2019). Codes developed for the codebook were reviewed with the committee chair, who was consulted with prior to revisions. The PI consulted the scholarly literature, comparing findings with the literature for a more comprehensive understanding of the themes as they were developed.

Confirmability

Strategies to achieve confirmability include reflexivity and triangulation (Forero et al., 2018). A reflective journal was maintained throughout the study, allowing the

PI to check personal perspectives and biases and ensure that the reported results reflect the survivors' experiences and not the PI's own imposed interpretations (Whittemore et al., 2001). Memos maintained in MAXQDA, the reflective journal, and the audit trail can be used as a form of triangulation to validate the data (Forero et al., 2018).

Transferability

Maximum variation sampling extends the degree to which the results may be transferred to other settings (Forero et al., 2018). However, this study sought individual experiences to provide insight into areas of prevention and intervention that were unknown; the goal was not to achieve data saturation but to obtain an in-depth understanding of survivors' experiences at a single university.

This study explored female survivors' experiences of college SV. The study sample came from Instagram, a social media site. The data used for this study were comprised of SV experiences shared by women survivors. The data were uploaded to a qualitative analysis software application and coded according to the established qualitative descriptive methodology. Themes were constructed and examined within the SEM.

Summary

Chapter Three outlined the methodology of this qualitative descriptive study. The chapter discussed the methodology, rationale, study setting, and protection of human subjects. Further this chapter describes the data, data analysis strategies, and final study sample (n = 384). Achievement of trustworthiness and rigor through credibility, dependability, confirmability, and transferability conclude this chapter.

Chapter 4: Findings

The purpose of the study was to describe the stories of college women and their experiences of SV in the context of the socioecological model (SEM). The long-term goal is to inform prevention and intervention strategies at all levels of the SEM. This chapter presents the results of the analysis of 891 Instagram posts. Analysis of the final study sample, 384 women's stories of college SV, revealed seven themes, including subthemes, that represent the experiences of the survivors. The chapter concludes with a summary of the findings.

Data Findings and Analysis

The following discussion represents the experiences of SV shared by college women survivors. Because of the nature of the data shared on the social media platform, demographic information such as age, racial/ethnic identity, and economic status were not available. Half of the survivors included the year of their enrollment at the university in their story. Within the sample, survivors 74.5% (n = 143) who shared the year of enrollment were freshman, 20.3 % (n = 39) were sophomores, 5.2% (n = 10) were juniors, and 1.6% (n = 3) seniors. The year of enrollment is unknown for 49.2 % (n = 189) of the women.

Social media data do not have the depth that researchers would find in interview data; clarification and follow-up questions were not possible. Nonetheless, seven themes were constructed that represented the experiences of college SV as described by survivors. Each theme and subtheme are discussed using direct quotations from the survivors' stories. The survivors' stories have been quoted exactly, without changing the spelling or language. The following themes were constructed from these stories:

1) Location Matters

2) Against My Will

3) Response and Resistance Strategies

4) The Consequences of Rape Culture in the Aftermath

5) Impact of Trauma on Health and Well-Being

6) Survivors Preventing, Advocating, and Educating

7) Survivors Solidarity, Supporting, and Healing

The SEM provided a strong conceptual base and was useful in framing the study. However, no individual story could be categorized as relevant to only one level of the SEM during the analysis process, as each story described multiple influencing factors at each level of the SEM. This aligns with the SEM's core concept: multiple levels of influence driving behaviors/actions.

Thematic Findings

Location Matters

Over half of the stories (54 %, n = 209) described the physical environment where the women experienced college SV. This theme and subsequent subthemes were constructed from survivors' descriptions of the social and shared spaces in which college SV had occurred. This theme has two subthemes: *community environment* and *campus environment.* In this study, the social norms described by survivors included attending off-campus parties and frequenting local community bars. The survivors described the social and shared spaces in which they experienced college SV by, for instance, naming the bar, associated fraternity house, or dorm building. These spaces were on the university campus or in the surrounding community.

Community Environment. A vast majority of the survivors shared that their experiences of SV had occurred at local bars, fraternity houses, or off-campus student housing. Survivors described off-campus settings by naming the bar or fraternity or offering street locations. For example, one survivor shared, "this was one of my first few times downtown, I didn't know where I was, it was the middle of the night." One survivor used the name of a street when describing her off-campus experience: "I remember waking up in a pool of blood in a random apartment. It was my first week at (X University) and had no idea where I was. I remember stepping onto Washington Street and crying." Another example of how survivors described SV that occurred off-campus is seen here: "Since he lived downtown, he and his friend invited us to his apartment to hang out." Events occurring after a house party were shared by another survivor: "He left me laying on the ground outside in a woody area." After returning to campus, she received medical care from the university's emergency medical services. Survivors also referred to "downtown," an off-campus location. For example, "I was drinking with friends in downtown...... We were in a bar when a guy approached me."

For those survivors who experienced college SV at a fraternity house, explicit reference to the associated fraternity was often included in their story, as shown in the following group of quotes: "We were at their house (TEP) for a mixer"; "My first semester at a party in (Dchi), I was at their basement"; "one of the first parties i had gone to (TEP)"; "I was at a party at APES"; "my friends and I went to a party at kappa sig";

and "My sophomore year I was drunk at SAE." Similarly, several survivors who experienced college SV at a bar named the bar when sharing their story, as in, "I was at the Rat and had lost my friends in the crowd." Another survivor experienced SV while "at the second Halloween party at Liquid Nightclub." In some instances, survivors described stopping at a bar prior to a fraternity house, as is the case with this survivor: "I went to APES after a night out at the bars."

Campus Environment. The survivors described student and Resident Assistant's (RA) dorm rooms, buildings, and (professors') offices as places and spaces where SV had occurred. Experiences of SV frequently occurred in the same building—even in the same hallway—where the survivor lived. When describing their experiences on campus, survivors frequently included the events leading up to the SV. Some survivors described having spent time with the perpetrators in their dorm room, for example, studying: "we would go through lines at each other's dorm." Other experiences occurred in dorms rooms while watching TV or hanging out with the perpetrator. One survivor shared, "he asked me to come hang out with him in his dorm. I wasn't interested in hooking up, and I explicitly let him know I was just coming to study/watch a movie."

A survivor who received a ride back to campus with her perpetrator shared, "I tried to tell him where I lived on campus, he just said he'd take me back to his room instead because it was closer." Another survivor wrote, "I was kissing this guy (at a bar) who I vaguely knew from my dorm." Later that evening, she blacked out. Her next memory was waking up in his dorm room. One survivor experienced SV in her building after returning from "downtown" and attending a party down the hall from her dorm room. Two survivors in the study shared that their experiences of SV had occurred in an

RA's room. Survivors also shared experiences of SV that occurred in professional spaces on campus, including two in (professors') offices on campus.

Against My Will

Describing experiences that occurred against their will was expressed as an overarching theme in survivors' stories, as this appeared in the majority (77.5%, n = 297) of the survivors accounts of SV. This theme and subsequent subthemes reflect the multiple and varied characteristics of how women experienced college SV. Each subtheme was constructed from survivors' accounts of their experience, and each reflects the power imbalances and gendered norms that influence college SV. The subthemes are as follows, *incapacitation, coerced, powerless and held hostage,* and *non-consensual videos and photos.*

Incapacitation. The vast majority of survivors' stories that described the characteristics of the SV included details of incapacitation from alcohol or drugs. Survivors shared experiences in which they "blacked out" and woke up confused and disoriented, recalling different portions of the assault. For instance, one survivor described waking up confused and finding someone she did not know in her dorm room. Some survivors describe coming in and out of awareness during the assault. One survivor who woke up while being assaulted shared, "At some point I just passed out on his bed and woke up with him inside of me. I don't know how it happened." Survivors shared that being incapacitated they were not only unable to consent but unable to resist sexual contact. For example, "I couldn't move or speak or lift my head off the bed." Another survivor shared, that she could not have consented to sex as she was "blackout drunk."

Multiple survivors described being unknowingly drugged and subsequently incapacitated, as in, "We had all taken a cup of whatever it was the frat was serving, and within 5 minutes the room was spinning and still my memory of what happened is only in bits and pieces, which is why I believe either the punch was spiked, or someone slipped something into my cup." Another survivor recalled blacking out after one cup of punch: "I am not a lightweight and I've never blacked out before. I woke up the next morning in a guys cloths I didn't recognize." After waking up on the floor of a fraternity house, a survivor who sought medical care shared her experience: "They told me I was drugged and that they found semen, so I was in fact raped… I was so scared and confused."

Coercion. Some survivors shared their experiences of being manipulated, pressured, or worn down by perpetrators. Survivors offered several descriptions of coercion via pressure, as in, "He proceeded to pressure me saying 'I made him hard' and 'I was the one who instigated making out and flirting with him.'" Another survivor shared how the perpetrator responded when she said no: "He tried to guilt me by telling me how he thought I was cool, but I wasn't being cool at that moment, that he thought I was different, and that it'd be rude to give him blue balls." Some survivors who described coercive tactics by perpetrators shared that they "gave in" or "caved" to the pressure so the perpetrator would leave them alone. For example, one survivor explained, "He kept trying until I got tired of saying no and just gave in. I had sex with him even though I didn't really want to just to get him to leave me alone." Another survivor, whose story also reflected this theme, shared, "I felt a ton of pressure to progress even though I wasn't ready to, like I was a tease or something for not being ready… He would also insult me and my appearance, say I was being awkward or make me feel more uncomfortable than I already was." After persistent begging, one survivor, who agreed to go into the perpetrator's room, described how the situation quickly escalated: "he was really aggressive and immediately threw me against a wall." Few survivors also shared how they were coerced into sex so they could get home, such as this survivor:

> He said he would call the cab if I had sex with him again so he told me he called it and while we waited for it he made me do several more sexual acts and I just wanted to get home so I did it.

Powerless and Held Hostage. Several survivors described the perpetrator's use of physical restraint, physical force, or a physical barrier to force sexual contact. Using their bodies, perpetrators "pinned" and "held" survivors down, as described by this survivor:

> He held my body in place so that I couldn't try to squirm away when I was saying stop and couldn't even move. It felt as though this went on for hours and hours and I couldn't do anything about it.

Another survivor described how each time she cried or said "no," the perpetrator "would shove my face down into the bed with his hand over my mouth or hold me down by my neck." One survivor described being restrained, feeling "completely immobile… as he carried me outside the frat house and into the woods behind."

Another finding related to this theme, described by many survivors, was how the perpetrator "pushed," "pulled," or "held" the survivors' hands or head toward their penis. For instance, one survivor described how he was "forcibly grabbing my hand to place on his penis." Other survivors shared being restrained by physical barriers such as a locked door. For example, one survivor wrote, "I tried opening the door but he had locked me in," while another survivor shared that she was led to the perpetrator's bedroom, where he "then locked the door behind me."

Nonconsensual Photographs and Videos. Some survivors shared their experiences of non-consensual video recording and photographs. They gave various accounts of how they discovered the photos or recordings occurred. For instance, one survivor "noticed a flash," another spotted "a camera propped at the end of the bed," and another shared how she "suddenly noticed someone was recording" her. Many survivors shared that a third party recorded the SV such as this survivor, "I noticed a flash coming from the corner of my eye and realized his friends were recording/ taking a picture of him raping me."

Several survivors learned that they had been recorded when a friend or acquaintance informed them. One survivor described being approached by a friend who told her that "there was video proof" of her SV experience. Another shared that after "word got around," she learned she had been recorded. Having learned this from someone else, she was left wondering who else had seen the recording and who would see it in the future. One survivor who confronted the perpetrator after learning that she had been recorded shared:

> One day, one of his suite mates (also my friend) informed me that he and the rest of his suite had been sent a video/videos of me and (perpetrator) having sex in a group snap. I confronted him about it and he said that no one could see my face so what was the problem.

Survivors who were recorded without consent expressed feeling anxious and helpless knowing that there were recordings that could later be shared, as described by this survivor: "To this day I don't know if the images have been deleted." One survivor who disclosed her experience with nonconsensual photos to a formal support person was first asked if she had used "protection" and was then told, "if you are really worried you can go to university police department and they will force them to delete the photos."

Response and Resistance Strategies

This theme was constructed from the survivors (37.4 %, n = 111) accounts of how they responded to or resisted the perpetrator. Many survivors describe verbally resisting the perpetrator by using clear and forceful communication, such as "no" or "stop." Others shared that they had "yelled loudly" or "screamed" for help. While some survivors shared the diversion strategies they used, such as, "I am on my period," "I have to meet friends," and "I have a boyfriend."

Multiple survivors described responding to the perpetrators with physical force, such as pushing the perpetrator and trying to pull away. A survivor shared, "I tried pushing him off but I was pinned down." One survivor described how she tried to push the perpetrator away, however he just became more aggressive and would not stop: "I tried to pull away, but he wouldn't let me." Another survivor shared, "I tried stopping his hands from reaching for my chest, or trying to unzip my pants he wouldn't stop." Some survivors described using both verbal and physical resistance strategies to stop the perpetrator such as this survivor: "I continued to try and push him and yell while he continued." Survivors shared feeling ignored, overpowered, defeated, and powerless despite their efforts to resist the perpetrator.

Moreover, some survivors shared that they were "paralyzed with fear," "left without a choice," "frozen," and felt "powerless" during the attack/violence, unable to fend off the perpetrator. One survivor shared, "I was paralyzed with fear I didn't say or move, and he did what he did to me." Another survivor shared that while in the perpetrator's room, she "didn't know how to fight back, he was large and aggressive....I didn't know what would happen if I did try to push him off of me. I felt powerless." One survivor described an "out of body experience where I just froze" after hearing a condom package ripped open. She further reflected, "Looking back, he just entered I me with no consent and I felt so scared and ashamed the whole time to even try to fight back." After repeatedly telling a perpetrator "no" while he was forcing himself on her, another survivor shared, "I resigned myself to staring at a wall and disassociating until it was over."

The Consequences of Rape Culture in the Aftermath

Many survivors' stories (58%, n = 222) described the aftermath of their experiences of SV in the context of a culture that supports harmful norms and attitudes, excuses perpetrators, and promotes SV. Rape culture influenced how survivors *processed and named the trauma*, led to *self-blame*, experienced *victim-blaming*, and guided their thoughts on *disclosing* their experience. Each of these is a subtheme of this finding.

Processing and Naming the Trauma. Several survivors' stories described how they processed their experiences of college SV. While making meaning of their experiences, survivors described the ways they minimized and normalized their experiences. For example, one survivor shared that initially, she viewed her experience "at the time" as "normal gross guy behavior and let it go." Another survivor, who was a virgin at the time of her experience, shared, "I convinced myself everything was okay." Because it was her first sexual experience, she considered it to be the norm. A survivor who was forcefully coerced shared, "well he didn't rape me so I'm fine. I don't have the right to be traumatized over it, but I am."

While at her first college party, a survivor wrote that she experienced behavior that was "uncomfortable…but I figured this was normal behavior at a college party." After reading others' stories she "realized" that what she experienced was SV. Another survivor who began processing her experience after reading other survivors' stories shared,

> He didn't even ask because he knew I was so drunk and was barely even conscious, he just did it….. seeing all of these statements have made me realize that what happened to me was not okay, even though I shrugged it off to be.

Several survivors described how they processed their experience when alcohol was involved. For instance, one survivor shared how she initially excused the perpetrator because she was "the one blacked out." Reflecting on her own experience, another survivor shared how processing her experience was constant, and although she was intoxicated, she reminded herself that "it wasn't my fault… it should not have happened."

Some experiences shared by survivors began as consensual sexual contact. This created a conflict in how the survivors' processed their experience. For example, one survivor shared, "I consented, so I feel like I can't claim sexual assault, but after saying 'no, 'please,' 'stop,' 'I can't breathe,' I'm left wondering if what I experienced transformed into an act of assault." Another survivor shared that she had "repressed" memories and believed that there was nothing wrong with what had happened because "it started off consensual." One survivor shared that she initiated "kissing" but nothing more, yet she was still unsure if it was SV.

Many stories mentioned the length of time survivors took to process the trauma. After one year, one survivor learned that she was not alone after reading others' SV stories. She explained, "I've never really known how to feel about this situation, I still don't know how to feel." Another survivor reported the perpetrator one year after the SV. She shared that after one year she "processed this attack as rape." One survivor, who shared that she had experienced SV twice, remarked, "It took me a long time to even be able to say the words 'I was raped twice'. It's still hard and it's been almost 4 years."

Self-Blame. Some survivors described how they placed the responsibility of avoiding or stopping the SV on themselves. For instance, a survivor questioned her actions, wondering if she "gave him the wrong impression." Survivors also blamed themselves for not "resisting adequately," as described by this survivor: "Like if i just fought back, if i just tried a little harder, it wouldn't have happened.... i felt like it was my fault." Again, this survivor shared that she "wasn't strong enough" to get the perpetrator off her. Some survivors wondered whether their actions had led to the SV. For example, one "questioned if I invited him." The same sentiment was shared by this survivor: "I always just thought I was dancing too provocatively or dressed a certain way so I deserved it." Such reactions are consistent with a culture where gatekeeping and rape avoidance are the responsibility of women. One survivor described the self-imposed changes she had made since to avoid another experience of SV: "I no longer wear dresses or skirts, and cant use bathrooms at parties alone." In some instances, survivors expressed regret over drinking and felt that the SV was the result of their drinking. For example, a survivor "blamed herself" for not only drinking but "entering into an inebriated state."

Victim-Blaming. Survivors' who disclosed their experiences received a range of responses. In addition to blaming the survivors for the SV, formal and informal supports responded in distracting and dismissive ways to disclosure. One survivor shared her experience with the university and law enforcement:

> I called the cops and went in for a rape kit and the cops and school said it'd be better for my court case not to test for roofies because the lab tests may show the amount of alcohol in my system which would go against me.

Another survivor was asked what she had been wearing during the attack when she gave her statement and if she "had moaned to give off pleasure." During a sorority chapter meeting, a survivor shared that a university representative told a group of college women "it would be our fault for going to an off-campus frat, and that we were just asking to be assaulted at that point."

It was common for survivors to describe the reactions they received from friends after disclosing. For instance, one survivor was told to stop drinking so much "so that stuff like this" would not happen again. Another survivor who was blamed for the violence because she had been drinking, shared "In the morning, my friends blamed me for being too drunk." A survivor shared that her female friend responded to her by telling her that she, the survivor, should have behaved differently: "you shouldn't have gone out alone with just guys." After finally "having the courage" to disclose, another survivor shared how disappointed she was when her friends called her a "liar" and "a tease." One survivor reported being called a "party pooper," and several were told that their experience "wasn't a big deal," that they were being "dramatic" and "overreacting," and they were treated as if they, the survivors, were the ones who had done something wrong.

Survivors shared the responses that they received that excused the behavior of the perpetrator, shifting blame to the survivor. After disclosing to friends a survivor shared that they responded by insisting "I must have led him on somehow." Another survivor shared her friends responded by telling her that she gave the perpetrator the "wrong impression" and should have "given him clearer signals." Shifting blame was also done by perpetrators. For example, a perpetrator blamed the survivors "for 'allowing' him to do all that stuff to me in the first place." Another survivor shared that that the perpetrator expressed anger towards her for "giving him a bad rep" as an "abuser."

Considering Disclosure. Survivors described various rationales, rooted in societal norms, that shaped how they thought about, and whether they would disclose, their experience. A few shared why they felt that they would not be believed by their peers or campus authorities. For instance, one survivor wrote, "I never pressed charges because no one would believe me if I left with a guy willing." Another woman shared that, because she had drunk alcohol, "I didn't think anyone would in the university system would believe me," and so she thought she would be humiliated. One survivor described wondering whether the perpetrator would be believed over her because of her costume and because she had been drinking. Few survivors expressed concerns that they would be punished for drinking if they disclosed. A student-athlete survivor shared, "there were no resources I could utilize without simultaneously getting in trouble for drinking."

The social implications associated with disclosure were described in multiple survivor stories. The survivors expressed concern that peer groups would judge them negatively rather than blame their perpetrator. One woman shared, "I didn't want to be seen as that girl that got him in trouble." Another survivor expressed the same sentiment:

> I realized that ultimately the system has failed us so many times and we still are a part of a culture that will find fault in our actions rather than directing the conversation about the character of the individual who committed this act of abuse.

The following statement, from another survivor, underscores the overall futility expressed by survivors who felt the potential benefits of disclosing would not be worth the social consequences:

> There is no concrete result...There is no money involved and the only outcome is pure pain and embarrassment. She'll lose the majority of her friends and she'll lose her reputation...It is an awful process that takes months... I feel hopeless even now.

Impact of Trauma on Health and Well-Being

This theme was constructed from the survivors (31%, n = 119), descriptions of the psychological, physical, and academic impact they suffered from the trauma of SV. Survivors described a range of immediate and long-term psychological impacts, physical injuries and reproductive health implications, and academic consequences from the trauma.

Psychological Impact. The *psychological impacts* described by survivors were extensive and severe. They reported panic attacks, anxiety, depression, post-traumatic stress disorder, nightmares, and suicidal ideation that had not been present prior to their experiences of college SV. These symptoms often lasted months or years. Several months after her experience, one survivor shared, "I still dream about it, scared he could've done worse." Other survivors developed insomnia, and multiple survivors reported experiencing anxiety that had not been there prior to the SV. For instance, one survivor shared, "I developed PTSD that caused insomnia, extreme anxiety, and a black out whenever I would drink."

Seeing the perpetrator on campus or in class triggered various emotional responses from numerous survivors. For instance, one woman shared, "I get extremely nervous when I see (perpetrator) or other members of the frat." A survivor who experienced SV in her dormitory shared how she lived in fear every day knowing that the perpetrator also lived there. One survivor described her reaction when seeing the perpetrator walk into her classroom as follows: "I felt like I could not breathe," and she became extremely anxious.

In their stories, survivors described how the experience had affected their romantic and intimate relationships. Some survivors began to have difficulty trusting others, specifically men. Others described feeling "disgusted" at the thought of being touched by a man. One woman shared that she was unable to have sex even if it was consensual, and another experienced panic attacks during "consensual relations." Another survivor did not have sex for an "entire year" and was still unable to sleep unless her bedroom door was locked.

Physical Injuries and Reproductive Health. *Physical injuries* inflicted by the perpetrator were common in many survivors' stories. The most commonly reported were pain and bruising; a few survivors suffered bites or cuts. Survivors often noticed bruising the following day with variations in the extent and location. In addition to the varying degree of injury, the length of time survivors described pain and discomfort related to the violence ranged from days up to a year. One survivor shared, "I was raw and bleeding for weeks. It hurt to walk. It hurt to wear tight pants." After sustaining a vaginal tear, another survivor experienced pain and bleeding for a year. Some survivors described extensive bruising and pain:

> the bruising was so severe that I couldn't sit comfortably. I had blankets of dark bruising on both my upper thighs/ass 10 inches in circumference, my jaw and eyes were bruised and swollen, and my ears had bruised on the inside from being crushed against the side of my head by his hand.

Few of the survivors shared they used emergency contraception because the perpetrator did not use a condom, such as this survivor, "I had to drain my bank account to buy $50 plan b from Walmart." Additionally, some shared that they later learned they contracted an "STD" from the perpetrator.

Academic Consequences. The survivors also described the academic consequences they faced after experiencing college SV. A few specifically mentioned missing exams and reviews, while others shared that they had skipped classes or completely stopped going to class, such as this survivor: "I never went back to class and just stayed in my room for the rest of the semester." Some survivors describe disengaging from the campus community all together. One survivor wrote that she became disengaged from activities that she had previously enjoyed. Some survivors left the university by "transferring out" shortly after their experiences such as this survivor who just started her sophomore year "I ended up transferring." When survivors described transferring to another university often, they shared that they continued to have difficulty academically in the new setting. One survivor that left the university described the profound impact SV has had on her life: "I left (X university) my second semester sophomore year because I never felt safe there again. I lost my scholarship all my friends and still have not finished my college degree."

Survivors Preventing, Advocating and Educating

The theme survivors preventing and educating, was evident in survivors' stories (14%, n = 56). Survivors' express sharing their stories to prevent SV or to warn others, to advocate for institutional change, and to challenge social norms. Many survivors expressed hope that sharing their stories on Instagram would prevent others from experiencing SV, as expressed by this survivor: "All I want is for this to never to happen to another girl." After reading others' stories, several survivors learned they were not alone; others had had similar experiences, and so these survivors were then moved to share their own stories as well to increase awareness. One survivor wrote, "Seeing other girls share their story about (named perpetrator) makes me feel the need to come forward." Another survivor shared, "the fact that my experiences aren't at all isolated incidents, and now that I am seeing that sexual harassment and assault are not only recurring but common occurrences at (X university), I think it may benefit others to share."

Many survivors' stories advocated for institutional action and change. In terms of prevention education, one survivor recommended that the university "give a better education" about "assault" to new students. Advocating for survivor justice, one survivor wrote, "The institution needs to be held accountable for assaults that occur on and off campus. We need advocacy for change and policy reform at the institutional level. Times up!" Another survivor called on the university to stop SV from being an "underground initiation to college." Other survivors shared that they hoped their stories would create change at the university and within the student population. To prevent SV at the university, one survivor shared, "We need to demolish rape culture in Greek life, especially the underground organizations."

Several survivors used the Instagram platform to educate others on aspects of SV, reflecting upon the social norms and societal messages surrounding SV. One survivor described the impact of her trauma and encouraged others to "support your friends that have survived something like this." Another survivor encouraged peers to support survivors, not perpetrators: "Please believe in the survivors… Please stand by them and don't continue being friends with their assaulter even after they come to you with their story." Another survivor addressed the cultural norms that excuse male perpetrator behavior: "Women are more than our bodies. Men are more than their base impulses." Similarly, this survivor spoke to cultural norms and societal messages:

> I urge you to believe victims….I should not have to tell you i barely drank that night, explain i didn't mean to wear easy access clothing that night, and show you the scars on the back of my leg for you to begin to believe what I am telling you.

Survivors Solidarity, Supporting, and Healing

This theme encompasses how survivors (13.5%, n = 52) acknowledged and disclosed their experience, sought support, supported others, and expressed their solidarity with other survivors. Several survivors shared that they had not disclosed their experiences prior to sharing their story on Instagram such as this survivor, "I have never told anyone this story before." Another survivor, who had "suppressed" the memory, found strength from other survivors' sharing and, in turn, shared her own story of college SV. Other survivors shared that they had told close friends but no one else prior to sharing on Instagram. For example, "I haven't told anyone this story aside from my few best friends, but today I am speaking up."

Survivors expressed gratitude for the space to share their stories, and how they now felt supported and heard. For instance, this survivor said, "many thanks to this account for giving survivors a place to speak and feel heard. I appreciate you so much." Another survivor thanked others for giving her the courage to "speak up and for giving all girls at (X university) a platform to speak up." The topic of anonymity was present in several survivor stories, as in, "I'm still working on healing but saying it even anonymously helps so thank you so much for creating this platform."

Seeing other survivors post their stories helped some survivors name their experience: "Hearing other people's stories has allowed me to call this aggressive behavior what it really is, sexual assault." Another survivor shared how hard it had been to name her experience as SV but explained that seeing other survivors' sharing had "helped" her acknowledge her experience, "feel less alone, and afraid to tell people." One survivor, who thanked others for sharing, reflected on feeling alone: "reading these stories I feel like I'm not alone."

Often, survivors' stories offered messages of support for other survivors, such as this one: "I am so inspired by all the survivors who came forward - your strength and bravery inspire me every day. You're not alone." Speaking to other survivors about blame, one survivor shared, "it is not your fault. I often forgot this truth on my road to recovery," and, similarly, "it's never your fault and you are never asking for it." Showing solidarity with other survivors was part of the survivors' message, as in, "we are strong and important we can get through this together." Another survivor reminded others that they are "braver and stronger than their assaulters." By sharing their stories openly, survivors formed a collective voice that enabled them to find strength in the realization that they were not alone.

This chapter presented findings from the analysis of 891 posts on Instagram. The study data were analyzed in an iterative five-cycle inductive and deductive process to answer the following research questions: How do college women describe college SV experiences within a socioecological framework of intrapersonal, interpersonal, institution, community, and societal factors, and how may women's college SV experiences inform college SV prevention and intervention programs? The thematic findings of the final study sample, 384 female college SV survivors' stories, are described.

Chapter 5: Discussion

Chapter Five offers a synthesis of the study's findings, guided by the socioecological model, and integrates them into the existing literature. The limitations of the study, implications for practice, and suggestions for future research conclude this chapter. The SEM, which guided this qualitative descriptive research study, is a health behavior model that incorporates multiple levels of influence. According to the model, an individual's well-being depends on complex relations between their immediate settings, formal and informal social structures, societal norms, and institutional patterns (Bronfenbrenner, 1977).

The purpose of this study was to examine survivors' experiences through the lens of the SEM to provide an in-depth understanding of college SV as described by female survivors. A qualitative descriptive study design was utilized to accomplish two research aims. First, this study described the lived experiences of female survivors of SV at one large public university in the northeast. Second, this study examined the survivors' experiences of SV framed within the SEM.

The data for this study were extracted from a single account on the social media site Instagram, created by one or more SV activist(s). The data were comprised of moderator posts and SV experiences at a single university, shared by women survivors. After the data were extracted, they were uploaded to a qualitative analysis software application, analyzed, and coded according to established qualitative descriptive methodology. The data were analyzed in an iterative five-cycle inductive and deductive process. The analysis revealed seven themes, each of which included subthemes, related to the experiences of female college SV survivors; these were explicated in Chapter Four.

Problem Statement

Despite the activist-inspired motivation for change and federal compliance mandates, the prevalence of SV on college campuses remains a complex and persistent public health problem. Since the first prevalence study by Koss et al. (1987) prevalence of college SV has not decreased but has increased; currently it is estimated one in five female student experience college SV. Researchers have estimated the economic burden of this preventable public health problem to be over three trillion dollars (Peterson et al., 2017; Potter et al., 2018), and the effects of college SV on survivors may persist for years, altering entire life trajectories (Potter et al., 2018).

Prevention programs have proliferated, developed by researchers, colleges, and external organizations, although none have demonstrated a reduction in the prevalence of SV (Mujal et al., 2019; C. Ullman, 2020; Worthen & Wallace, 2018). Women who have experienced college SV have had little voice in developing or evaluating college SV prevention programs. Moreover, studies show SV survivors want the opportunity to share their experiences and contribute to violence prevention (Bloom et al., 2022; R. Campbell & Adams, 2009; Jaffe et al., 2017). Understanding the context where college SV occurs as described by survivors, provides a valuable contribution to developing college SV prevention education and programs established to support survivors. The thematic findings of the study in relationship to the literature will be discussed next.

Summary of Thematic Findings and the Literature

First, this study described the characteristics of the sample in respect of the data shared by participants. Because of the nature of the data, demographic information such as age, racial/ethnic identity, and economic status were unavailable. Half of the participants included the year of their enrollment when describing their experience. Within the sample, of those who shared the year of enrollment, 74.5% (n = 143) were freshmen, 20.3 % (n = 39) were sophomores, 5.2% (n = 10) were juniors, and 1.6% (n= 3) were seniors. Similarly, Cantor (2017; 2020) reported findings from the AAU Campus Climate Survey, which suggest SV prevalence declines based on year of enrollment in college. Research on college SV has consistently shown that the risk of SV is greater during a woman's freshman year (Caamano-Isorna et al., 2018; Cantor et al., 2020; Cranney, 2015; Krebs et al., 2016).

Location Matters

This study found that physical environments where college women socially interact and live are a risk factor for college SV. Specifically, locations off campus (e.g., fraternity houses, bars, apartments) present a greater risk than those on campus (e.g., student and RA dorm rooms, buildings and (professor) offices). The social space presenting the greatest risk of SV identified in this study was off-campus fraternity houses, occupied by fraternities unrecognized by the university. Related literature sheds light on possible explanations for this finding. College SV research has consistently shown Greek life is a significant risk factor for college SV (Cranney, 2015; Marcantonio et al., 2020; Muehlenhard et al., 2017; Wiersma-Mosley et al., 2017). Studies that have looked at college SV risk in relation to Greek life compare fraternity membership to nonmembership (Seabrook, 2021). One study of college SV risk has examined attitudes of fraternity members in unofficial houses compared to those in official houses. Seabrook (2021) reported fraternity members with unofficial houses more strongly endorse intimate partner violence than members of official fraternities. This area of prevention is not well studied; therefore, this finding contributes valuable information to the body of knowledge on risk factors for, and prevention of college SV.

Additionally, several women experienced SV at local bars. Prior research has shown an association between off campus drinking and sexual coercion (Ehlke et al., 2019). Settings such as bars and nightclubs have been shown to significantly increase a woman's risk of SV (Graham et al., 2014; Savard et al., 2017). This finding supports prior research and contributes to college SV prevention literature.

Against My Will

Incapacitation. Consistent with previous research, alcohol was a factor in several survivors' experiences of SV (Caamano-Isorna et al., 2018; Ford et al., 2021). Participants overwhelmingly described experiencing SV while incapacitated due to alcohol or drugs. These results are consistent with multiple studies that have evaluated interrelationships of incapacitation and other known risk factors, such as Greek life and year of enrollment (Gilbert et al., 2019; Lasky et al., 2017).

The survivors often described being incapacitated as being in a semi-conscious or unconscious state, where they were confused, disoriented and in a fluctuating state of awareness during the assault. Study participants related incapacitation to an inability to consent to or resist sexual contact. A recent study supports this finding (Dardis et al., 2020). S.E. Ullman et al. (2020) reported that survivors described incapacitation from voluntarily drinking alcohol and from unknowingly being drugged. Results from Dardis et al. (2020) also indicate that incapacitation was a result of being unknowingly drugged. Findings in this subtheme, *Incapacitation,* also describe how unknowingly being drugged was not consistently associated with bars, parties, or drinking but also occurred in non-social settings. This finding is significant in terms of combatting societal norms that blame victims when alcohol or drugs are a factor in the violence. Furthermore, drug-facilitated SV in non-social settings is poorly understood and is an important consideration for future research.

Coercion. This study found that multiple participants experienced coerced SV. Within this study, perpetrators used language and behavior to exert power and control over the participants. Coercive tactics used by perpetrators included pressure, guilt, nagging, and criticizing the appearance and behavior of study participants in order for them to acquiesce to unwanted sexual contact. In some instances, participants who were off campus were coerced into sexual contact for transportation home. Overall, this study found that perpetrators' coercive tactics resulted in some form of sexual contact unwanted by the women. These findings support previous research (Dardis et al., 2020; Edwards et al., 2014; Munro-Kramer et al., 2022).

Powerless and Held Hostage. Study findings in this subtheme highlight the ways women described their experience of forced SV. This study found that tactics used by perpetrators included using their body to restrain women, the use of physical force to move the woman's head or hands toward their penis and locking doors to prevent women from leaving. Forced SV has been identified in studies measuring college SV prevalence (Cantor et al., 2020; Fisher et al., 2000). However, only one other study (Edwards et al.,

2014) identified forcefully pulling the survivor's hand or head near their penis (e.g., forced oral sex or forced masturbation) as a tactic used in SV by perpetrators. This subtheme supports previously reported research describing perpetrator tactics in forced SV (Cantor et al., 2020; Edwards et al., 2014; Fisher et al., 2000).

Nonconsensual Photographs and Videos. This study found that women were photographed or recorded without their consent, often without their knowledge. Findings showed that images were taken during forced SV and coerced sex, sometimes by a third party, and/or while participants were unconscious. Additionally, images were shared via group messages or apps (e.g., Snapchat, GroupMe). When describing how they learned, they had been recorded or photographed, participants reported seeing a camera flash or were informed by individuals that viewed the images the perpetrator distributed. This finding is similar to current research (Dardis & Richards, 2022) however, unlike prior studies (Dardis & Richards, 2022; Reed et al., 2016), this study did not find that all participants previously knew or were in a relationship with the perpetrator. Study participants reported immediate psychological distress upon learning of the nonconsensual photographs/videos, as described in prior research (Eaton et al., 2017). Additionally, participants described feeling anxious and helpless knowing the images could be disseminated at any time and could not be deleted. These findings suggest participants may experience secondary trauma from future dissemination of nonconsensual photographs/videos.

Nonconsensual image sharing (e.g., posting private photographs or videos) is a growing form of SV (Eaton et al., 2017) and is a strategy used by perpetrators to maintain coercive control over women (Dardis & Richards, 2022; Munro-Kramer et al., 2022;

Reed et al., 2016). Buiten (2020) suggested that the range of harm and impact on survivors from nonconsensual images is poorly understood. Further, various terms used to describe nonconsensual images (e.g., revenge porn, nonconsensual pornography, digital rape, image-based sexual abuse) limit the ability to capture the impact on survivors (Buiten, 2020). The findings from this study suggest there are additional variables/factors in the use of nonconsensual images related to college SV that are not well understood. Findings in this subtheme support current literature (Dardis & Richards, 2022; Eaton et al., 2017; Munro-Kramer et al., 2022; Reed et al., 2016) and add relevant new evidence to the literature. Additionally, our findings underscore the importance of trauma-informed SV prevention and intervention programs.

Response and Resistance Strategies

This study identified women's responses to perpetrators during an assault were verbal, physical, and emotionally self-protective. Participants often overtly resisted the assault by saying "no," yelling and screaming. Study participants attempted to physically resist the perpetrator by kicking, hitting, and pulling and pushing away. Prior research on women's response and resistance to SV supports this finding (Canan et al., 2022; Edwards et al., 2014; Orchowski et al., 2021).

This thematic finding revealed that participants responded to the assault by disassociating. This response was described as relating to feelings of fear and powerlessness. These findings agree with prior (Edwards et al., 2014) and recently conducted research that evaluated women's reactions during sexual assault (Canan et al., 2022). The process of freezing or disassociating serves to emotionally protect the survivor. When disclosing survivors are often judged on their behavior leading up to and during the assault (Canan et al., 2022). Therefore, research that normalizes the various responses to SV is an important contribution to the college SV literature.

The Consequences of Rape Culture in the Aftermath

Processing and Naming the Trauma. This study found participants did not initially name or acknowledge their experience as SV. This was despite the fact that their experience met the operational and legal definition of SV. Study participants described how they minimized the assault or characterized it as normal college behavior. Only after reading other survivor stories did the participants start to process their experience as SV. This finding suggests that rape myths, that support victim blaming and acceptance of violence against women, influence how survivors process their trauma and are prevalent on the college campus. Participants also described consent as a consideration in how they named their experience, suggesting that when women's experiences do not meet the stereotypical rape script it creates uncertainty in their perception of the event. This finding is supported by prior research (Dardis et al., 2020).

Previous studies have consistently shown that the involvement of alcohol also influenced how participants named their experience (Dardis et al., 2020; Wilson & Miller, 2016). One participant explained how she constantly reminded herself that whether or not she had consumed alcohol, it was not her fault. Overall, this subtheme finding overall suggests women are continually exposed to stigmatizing societal messages and inaccurate information regarding SV. The findings in this subtheme shed light on the factors that influence how survivors view and frame SV. The findings in this subtheme were consistent with previous research (Dardis et al., 2020; Huppin & Malamuth, 2020).

Self-Blame. Internalized social ideologies that place the onus of blame for SV on women was evident in many of the participants' stories. The study findings revealed participants placed blamed on themselves, rather than on the perpetrator, for the assault. Reasons for self-blame included not resisting the assault or being strong enough to effectively stop the perpetrator. The reasons described by participants reflect the social narrative surrounding gender norms; men being unable to resist their urges and women being responsible for stopping them (Seabrook et al., 2018). Alcohol was also a factor in self-blame as participants assigned blame to themselves if they had been drinking prior to the assault. Some participants associated SV with punishment for their actions. In this narrative, the perpetrators actions were excused because the survivor "deserved" what happened. This finding is supported in prior research that has examined rape myths (Canan et al., 2018; O'Neal, 2017), and self-blame has been identified in studies examining barriers to disclosure for survivors (Carey et al., 2018; Holland & Cortina, 2017; Zinzow & Thompson, 2011).

Considering Disclosure. Study participants overwhelmingly anticipated negative reactions from formal and informal sources of support when considering disclosure. Participants anticipated being blamed for the assault or not believed. This suggests the campus culture justifies and tolerates perpetrators' behavior while blaming victims. Participants associated negative responses with the context of events leading up to the assault, such as how they were dressed or dancing, or if they were consuming alcohol. This reflects a common rape myth, that women are "asking for it" or that their actions caused the assault based on culturally sanctioned messages about what is good, bad, normal or abnormal behavior.

Moreover, the analysis revealed that participants considered the social and personal implications of reporting (e.g., drinking violations, loss of friendships). Without an option for amnesty, participants who consumed alcohol were unable to report to formal sources without facing disciplinary action. When considering disclosure to friends, participants again described feelings that they would not be believed, causing them to lose friendships and damaging their reputations. These finding suggest that participants view their campus culture, and the broader society, as rape supportive, and this influenced their decision to report/disclose (even to friends). Prior research that has examined barriers to disclosure support the findings of this study (Canan et al., 2018; Sabri et al., 2019).

Victim Blaming. Study participants described a range of victim blaming responses from formal (e.g., law enforcement, health care providers, university officials) and informal support (e.g., friends, peers). My analysis found that friends' and peer groups' responses to disclosure assigned blame to the survivors and rationalized the behavior of perpetrators. Additionally, the PI found that blame for SV was assigned to survivors when alcohol was involved, by both formal and informal supports. For example, participants were advised to reduce their alcohol consumption in order to prevent future assault. Henry et al. (2022) reported similar findings in their study examining how intoxication levels impact perceptions of campus SV. Negative reactions to SV violence disclosures are detrimental to survivors and often result in poorer psychological outcomes (Edwards, Waterman et al., 2020; Hawn et al., 2018; Salim et al., 2022), which in turn increases the survivor's risk of revictimization (Hawn et al., 2018). These finding are useful to inform college SV intervention programs.

Impact of Trauma on Health and Well Being

Psychological Impact. This analysis found the psychological impact of trauma was a significant factor for survivors post-assault. Study findings revealed that panic attacks, anxiety, depression, post-traumatic stress disorder, eating disorders, nightmares and suicidal ideation that had not been reported prior were most often described by participants following the SV experience. This finding is supported in the literature (Cantor et al., 2020; Claydon et al., 2022; Dworkin et al., 2017; Eisenberg et al., 2016; Herres et al., 2018). Seeing the perpetrator in class or around the campus triggered an emotional response such as anxiety. Participants also reported that their interpersonal relationships were impacted by the violence; fear and mistrust influenced intimate (emotional and sexual) relationships. This finding is supported by current research (Georgia et al., 2018; Rothman et al., 2021).

Physical Injuries and Reproductive Health. Study participants described physical injuries resulting from the assault. Findings included minimal bruising, pain, extensive cuts and bruising, and vaginal tears. Pain and discomfort from the injuries lasted for several days up to one year. Some participants sought medical care for their injuries from the assault. These findings are similar to prior research conducted on physical injuries resulting from SV (Cantor et al., 2020). Participants in the study also reported contracting sexually transmitted infections from the perpetrator and others took emergency contraception to prevent pregnancy. These findings are supported in the literature (Cantor et al., 2020; Potter et al., 2018).

Academic Consequences. This analysis identified several academic consequences survivors faced after the assault. Participants shared they were late for classes and/or failed to attend classes, reviews, and exams. A few participants shared they stopped attending classes altogether, withdrew from college, or changed universities. These findings are supported by prior research (Brewer et al., 2018; Cantor et al., 2020; Patterson Silver Wolf et al., 2016; Potter et al., 2018). Additionally, study findings showed SV has consequences for survivors' futures as some participants lost their scholarships and did not complete their education. This supports prior research demonstrating the long-term impact of SV on survivors' academic careers (Banyard et al., 2017).

Survivors Preventing, Advocating, and Educating

Gaining perspectives from a variety of students and engaging student activists in decision making has been suggested to assist with SV prevention (McMahon et al., 2021). Sexual violence survivors on college campuses have used technological advances to amplify their voices, promote culture change, and connect with one another in response to the handling of SV by institutions (Bovill et al., 2021; Gronert, 2019; Marine & Trebisacci, 2018). Survivors want to help prevent others from experiencing SV (Scoglio et al., 2021). This study's findings support that survivors' want to prevent others from experiencing SV, a sentiment explicitly stated by several survivors.

Social media sites have become a forum for responding to SV, increasing awareness of the types of SV, and combating rape culture, each important in SV prevention. The social media platform was used by study participants to challenge social norms and societal messages that surround SV. This finding is supported in recent literature (Guidry et al., 2021; Maas et al., 2018). In addition, study participants described their motivations for sharing their experiences on social media, including informing others of risks and raising awareness of the prevalence of SV on campus. Further, study participants advocated for institutional change by calling on the institution to provide better education to incoming students, and to take accountability for SV that occurs on or off the campus. This thematic finding confirms existing knowledge in the literature surrounding survivor activism and advocacy (Bovill et al., 2021; Gronert, 2019; Marine & Trebisacci, 2018).

Survivor Solidarity, Supporting, and Healing

Prior research has shown that survivors infrequently disclose their experiences of SV (Halstead et al., 2017; Moylan et al., 2019). The findings in this study parallel prior research, as several participants had not previously disclosed their experience. However, the platform provided a supportive space where survivors were able to name and share their experiences of SV for the first time. Moreover, participants in this study shared they were able to disclose the SV to both formal and informal supports because of the strength and inspiration they gained from reading other survivors' stories of SV. Mendes et al. (2018) reported similar findings in their case study of digital activism. Participants in their study reported feeling supported and empowered after disclosing their assault. Research supports the notion that disclosure can be part of the healing process. Additionally, disclosure facilitates identification of important details of the context and characteristics of SV, to further inform prevention programs and intervention services.

Callender and Klassen (2020) reported that by interacting with the ME TOO movement survivors felt empowered and connected. Further, showing solidarity with other survivors' was an important component of participants' recovery. Several participants in this study expressed support and solidarity to fellow survivors, writing messages such as "your not alone." Additionally, survivors described feeling empowered and supported reading others shared experiences. Therefore, this thematic finding, supports prior research (Callender & Klassen, 2020; Halstead et al., 2017; Mendes et al., 2018; Moylan et al., 2019).

Implications of this Study

Practice Implications

This study's findings have practice implications for college SV prevention and intervention. Each campus community is unique, and prevention and intervention program development should take campus community structure and process into account to develop meaningful and relevant programming. Furthermore, this study's thematic findings elucidate the importance of including survivors' voices in college SV prevention program development and in interventions designed to mitigate harms to survivors.

The finding, *Location Matters* suggests that for SV prevention education to be effective, it must address the social and physical environments that facilitate social interaction on and off campus. Bystander prevention reframes SV as a community issue, clarifying that all members of the institution living on or off campus are accountable for preventing SV. Fraternities that are unsanctioned and reside off campus must be included in college SV prevention training. Further developing community partnerships and collaborating with local businesses to engage the surrounding community is suggested to strengthen prevention efforts. Community-based prevention programs have been designed for the public. Universities and local business owners collaborated in "Safer Bars" prevention, training staff to intervene as bystanders (McMahon et al., 2021). Reddy et al. (2022) presented a short informal, short video to a nonstudent population to challenge rape myths. Expanding SV education to include the surrounding community and collaborating in prevention and awareness events is suggested to improve both SV prevention and intervention.

This study's thematic findings, *Against My Will, Response and Resistance,* and *The Consequences of Rape Culture in the Aftermath* suggest addressing social norms and gender role expectations by integrating bystander prevention and empowerment and risk reduction prevention is required in order to provide a more comprehensive approach to college SV prevention is needed. Understanding the many and varied ways women experience SV is important to both prevention work and post assault intervention. Programs designed to support survivors would benefit from screening assessments that explicitly inquire about women's exposure to a full range of SV experiences (e.g., incapacitated, coerced, forced, nonconsensual photographs and video recordings). Participants described a range of tactics used by perpetrators of SV, and a range of ways in which they responded to perpetrators. Prevention education should provide women with multiple responses to SV, opportunities to practice with feedback, and reinforce that SV is <u>never</u> their fault. Providing prevention education to all members of the campus community on methods of SV perpetration, survivor reactions and responses, and rape myths versus reality will strengthen prevention programs. Both prevention education and intervention programs must include normalizing the multiple ways women respond to SV and challenge the unreasonable expectations of how women should respond. Further, prevention education should clarify that nonconsensual image sharing is not only inappropriate and distasteful behavior but is itself a form of SV and is illegal. To adequately support survivors, post assault support and intervention must address the repeated and profound long-term consequences survivors may face from repeated dissemination of nonconsensual images. Addressing this form of SV will enhance both prevention education and intervention programs intended to mitigate harm.

Colleges should offer a range of supportive services, beyond psychological and medical care, to survivors. Furthermore, services and programs designed to support survivors following an assault must include academic support. This was evident in the thematic finding *Impact of Trauma on Health and Well-Being*. However, research overwhelming shows the majority of women do not seek support following SV. Providing appropriate and trauma-informed support services to those who do experience SV will work towards changing the campus culture. A supportive environment may bring more women forward to disclose SV, more importantly discourage perpetrators.

This study emphasizes the importance of collecting institution-specific data to guide prevention education and services to support survivors. To achieve this, colleges must obtain input from survivors. In the thematic finding *Survivors Preventing, Advocating, and Educating* participants in this study expressed a desire to help prevent college SV. Women educated others on forms of SV and warned of risk factors. Including survivors in prevention and intervention will provide a trauma and violence informed approach to program development, providing opportunity for real change.

Research Implications

This analysis is one of few to examine survivors' stories of college SV qualitatively. Study findings highlight the physical environments in which college women socialize are a risk factor for college SV and are understudied. Further research is needed to clarify what features of the social environment, both on and off campus influence risk. Studies that evaluate ways in which the surrounding community and campus can work together to prevent college SV will inform prevention at the policy, community and institution level of the SEM. Additional research is required to evaluate not only Greek involvement, but the status of the fraternity or sorority as a factor in college SV risk. Institutional polices sanctioning fraternities may unknowingly work against SV prevention efforts if that fraternity continues to function, unaffiliated with the university (Seabrook, 2021).

Prior research has identified ambiguity in terminology used to determine college SV prevalence. Current research reporting prevalence (Cantor et al., 2020) of college SV does not include nonconsensual images, although it is a form of SV. Including nonconsensual images in prevalence studies will capture the extent of this form of SV. Further studies are needed to better understand the nature of and extent of harm this form of SV has on survivors in order to inform intervention programs intended to support survivors. Additionally, research is needed to determine the types of SV and extent of academic consequences.

Additional qualitative research is required to further understand the complexities involved in the survivors' experiences. Such research could inform the design of multilevel prevention and intervention programs and policies that are specific to individual college campuses. While the findings of this study highlight areas for intervention, further studies that comprise all members of the campus community are needed so that prospective interventions are designed to be accessible and appropriate for all members of the campus community.

Nursing Research. Scholars in the discipline of psychology, social work, criminal justice, women and gender studies, and sociology have been the lead investigators for college SV research. Nursing has an essential role in health and patient health outcomes. Further nurses are positioned in health care settings (e.g., emergency rooms, college health centers) where SV survivors who seek services are seen. Therefore, nursing is well suited to generate evidence to inform prevention of SV the care of survivors. Advancing the field of forensic nursing can be achieved by conducting studies that look at short and long-term health outcomes related to SV, associations between SV and chronic disease, and determining what support is most valued by survivors. Strengthening forensic nursing and forensic nursing education is critical to providing effective support and care to college SV survivors, preventing revictimization, and minimizing potential adverse health sequalae.

Policy Implications

This study demonstrates that SV is rooted in social structural factors that intersect across the social ecology. New York State is among the 50 U.S. states which have laws regarding nonconsensual images. Section 1401 of the Violence Against Women Act (VAWA), passed in October 2022 is the first federal law that addresses nonconsensual images and creates the National Resource Center on Cyber Crimes Against Individuals (The White House, 2022). However, neither VAWA nor state laws address the removal of nonconsensual pornographic material from online forums. Without a removal remedy, policy on nonconsensual image sharing does not address the profound long-term social and mental health consequences survivors face. Both federal and state laws need to address dissemination of nonconsensual images (State Revenge Porn Policy, n.d.) and the legal consequences for those who disseminate such material.

Provisions included in the reauthorization of the VAWA strengthen and modernize laws related to violence against women. Specifically, Title V, Sections 502 and 505 increase services and support for survivors. These provisions call for strengthening health care grant programs that respond to SV victims and authorize funding to establish a National Continuing and Clinical Education Pilot Program for sexual assault forensic examiners (117th Congress of the United States of America). Bipartisan support at the state and federal level is necessary to combat SV. However, states continue to create policies that inhibit post-assault care for survivors (e.g., restricting access to emergency contraception) and fail to create policies that support gender equality (e.g., childcare affordability, close gender pay gap, paid-family-leave programs). While expanding and strengthening healthcare services for survivors improves current available support, such services are overwhelmingly underused by survivors (Edwards, Ullman et al., 2020; Holland et al., 2021; McMahon et al., 2018; Mitra et al., 2021; Sabri et al., 2019). A federal and state policy response that supports gender equality and combats pro-sexual violence societal norms is required. When women are seen as equal and feel safe, supported, and heard, then rates of SV may decrease and women who have been assaulted may begin to consistently seek care.

Title III Section 303 of the VAWA authorizes added funding aimed at expanding awareness and prevention programs on college campuses, including support for institutional health centers and programs focused on dating violence. While added funding will provide colleges with the ability to expand current programs institutions need guidance on what programs decrease the prevalence of SV. Further, policy at the national level is needed to mandate colleges to do more than check a box. Colleges must provide prevention education that is empirically shown to decrease rates of SV. Prevention education should be given multiple times throughout the students enrollment at an institution.

The results of this study demonstrate a requirement for policies that expand awareness and prevention in the communities that surround the campus, and support campus and community partnerships. Funding is needed for public health campaigns that support educating and training in the general community beyond the campus to create public awareness of the wide range of women's SV experiences, and to show that any woman, regardless of risk, can experience SV. In the absence of a society that acknowledges every person is equal, SV will continue.

Finally, institutions with underground/unsanctioned fraternities must consider instituting polices that make joining such organizations a violation. Warning that such organizations exist is not sufficient to deter students from joining. Universities must issue sanctions against students that join such organizations. Furthermore, to address the status of Greek housing as private residences outside the jurisdiction of institutions local municipalities must consider adopting zoning ordinances, making occupation by unrecognized fraternities or sororities unlawful. Fraternity houses and membership are well established risks in college SV. It is imperative that we address this well known risk at the policy level of the SEM in order to have the greatest impact.

Application of the Socioecological Model

Framing women survivor stories in the SEM provided a nuanced understanding of the interactional phenomena related to college SV. Study participants described influencing factors related to college SV at each level of the model. Each thematic finding in this study supports the basic premise of the SEM; providing individuals with skills to promote health is ineffective if cultural norms and policies do not support health. For example, rather than one specific approach to prevention, colleges must foster an overall social environment that deters perpetrators and aggressive sexual behavior. Stigmatizing societal messages that women receive may become internalized, becoming an intrapersonal factor influencing how survivors process the assault. This was identified in participants' descriptions of self-blame.

According to the study findings, SV occurs as a result of both individual actions and societal and structural elements impacted by intersecting social locations. An important component in understanding behavioral influences is identifying the setting (e.g., physical environment or space) where the behavior occurs (McMahon, 2015; McMahon et al., 2021). The physical environment where participants experienced SV was primarily off campus, in the surrounding community. Campus SV prevention and response programs uniformly focus on intrapersonal and interpersonal factors and influences. Intrapersonal and interpersonal factors, however, can be influenced, positively or negatively by environmental context. Further research is required to examine how the physical environment influences college SV prevention and intervention. Application of the SEM to this study's findings created several opportunities to inform prevention and intervention program development (Figure 3).

Figure 3
Primary, Secondary, and Tertiary Approach to College SV Prevention

Primary Prevention	SEM Level	Secondary and Tertiary Prevention
• Policy/Laws creation or enforcement: zoning laws, higher insurance rates for Greek housing • Public health funding for SV prevention campaigns • Federal and State laws addressing removal of nonconsensual images • Social policies that promote gender equality	Policy Societal	• Public health funding for community campaigns: normalizing victim responses, anyone can be a victim consequences (e.g., medical, psychological, academic). • Federal mandates for law enforcement yearly education and training • Provide free health care, immediate and ongoing to survivors. • Funding victim advocate services and SANE training programs
• Institution and Community partnerships- address access to alcohol and other known risk factors in the community. • Training community members beyond the campus community to respond as active bystanders.	Community	• Screening for SV at local hospitals and outpatient clinics • Ongoing education for formal service (e.g., law enforcement health care) providers in the community on harmful responses to disclosure. • Community (and Campus) advocacy, disclosure response teams.
• Modification of institutional policies: violations for joining unrecognized fraternities • Prevention programing that addresses nonconsensual images. • Repeated staff/faculty education on SV prevention • Engaging students/survivors prevention program development	Institution	• Provide anonymous reporting options on and off campus • Provide supportive care beyond medical care (e.g., academic, psychological) • Health center screenings for all forms of SV, link survivors to resources • Repeated staff/faculty education on harmful responses to disclosure
• Decreasing the desirability of unrecognized fraternities: offering alternate options/group. • Education for healthy interpersonal and sexual relationships. • Peer leadership programs, prosocial modeling	Interpersonal	• Consistent messages from all levels starting at the top, SV is not tolerated • Training peers/peer groups on appropriate responses to disclosure. • Reinforce alcohol does not negate perpetrators responsibility.
• Integration of empowerment, response and resistance classes and bystander training. • Education on definitions of SV and consent, and dismantling gender norms, prevalence of violence against women	Intrapersonal	• Information on institution and community supports and services delivered around campus through poster campaigns and via social media sites

Strengths and Limitations

A strength of this study is the descriptive nature of the findings. Examining survivors' lived experiences is important for understanding the complexity and impact of college SV on survivors as well as the community. Descriptive research can better characterize the different types of SV, survivor responses and ways SV impacts the survivors, so that tailored prevention and intervention strategies can be developed. Studies have been designed to look at specific concepts related to college SV. Another strength of the study is the participants were not asked about their experiences related to research driven questions. In fact, women shared with other survivors what they chose to share from their experience. The experiences that women shared confirmed concepts and phenomena that have been found in previous research on college SV and provided new information. Therefore, this study adds to the SV literature contributing new findings to inform SV prevention and intervention.

Although social media allowed these survivors to freely share their experiences in a space deemed safe, the anonymous nature of the data was a limitation. Data used for the study were based on self-reporting and what the survivors chose to share from their experiences. Because of the nature of the data, an online platform with anonymous participants, the PI was unable to ask clarification questions or probe for additional information. Gender was inferred and survivor demographics were unavailable. In addition, the data were from one public university located in the northeast and therefore conclusions and/or recommendations may not be generalizable.

Conclusion

This study highlights how the involvement of survivors is critical to the development of effective prevention and intervention programs. Each campus community is unique, therefore programming development should take this into account in order to develop meaningful and relevant policies. The study's findings open several potential pathways to strengthen prevention and intervention programs and their evaluation. Preventing college SV requires a collaborative approach that includes campus and community partners. It is necessary to build community partnerships, where members of the community and campus representatives work together, in order to strengthen the response to those victimized. Intervention programs require a trauma-informed approach that supports survivors and minimizes the negative impact on their health and well-being. Furthermore, colleges must prioritize developing an approach to prevention that does not isolate men, involves the campus and surrounding community, and empowers women. Changing prevalent societal views surrounding college SV and survivors, alongside education and awareness that targets cultural norms that legitimize violence against women must begin at the policy level of the social ecology. A top down approach to prevention and intervention will have the greatest impact, reaching more individuals than an individual approach to prevention.

Finally, this study makes several contributions to the college SV literature. It provides insight into, and relevant knowledge of, college SV prevention programs and programs aimed to support survivors. It highlights the impact of societal norms, and the consequential trauma survivors face, from perspectives of the survivors. The findings emphasize the importance of including survivors in the design, outreach, interpretation and dissemination of SV prevention and intervention programs, assessing program efficacy, and informing future policy direction.

www.ingramcontent.com/pod-product-compliance
Lightning Source LLC
Chambersburg PA
CBHW051453290426
44109CB00016B/1743